Making Peace with Anxiety

VARSH PATEL

Making Peace with Anxiety

Copyright © 2020, Varsh Patel

Self-published
First printing, 2020
All rights reserved.

No part of this publication may be reproduced, stored in a retrieval system, stored in a database and/or published in any form or by any means, electronic, mechanical, photocopying, recording or otherwise, without the prior written permission of the publisher.

ISBN: 979-8-6685-8653-0

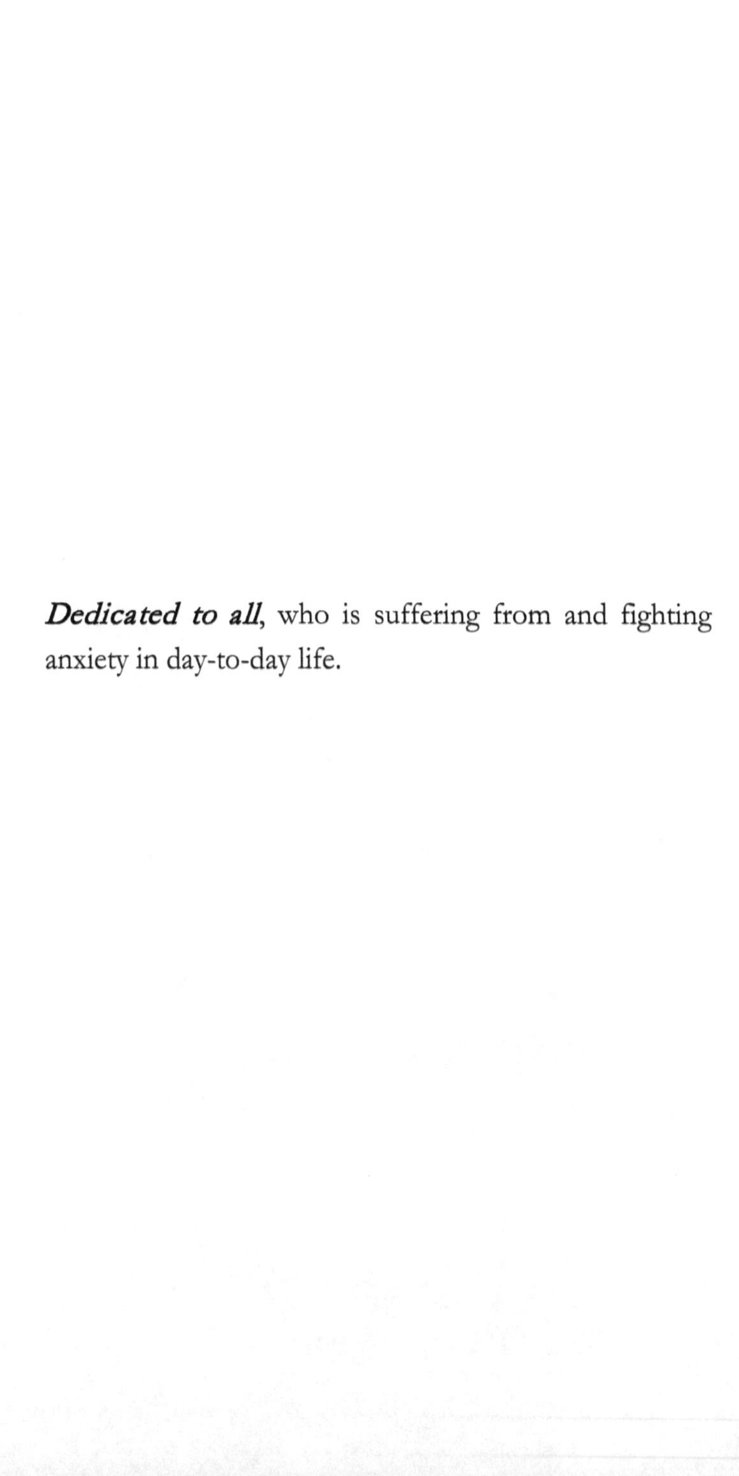

Dedicated to all, who is suffering from and fighting anxiety in day-to-day life.

In memory of, Late Shri Jayantibhai Patel – my hero, my dada.

I miss you.

CONTENTS

Starter Guide

This book is a self-help guide for understanding the basics of anxiety and learning the right strategies to deal with it. You will gain knowledge about the things that you might wonder about is only happening to you.

Always keep a notebook or your journal handy while you read this book so you can jot down your thoughts about various topics and strategies as you learn and try them out. Your notes will help you reflect on what you are learning and how your new skills can help you better cope with anxiety. There is only one way to make and learn automatic responses to your anxiety triggers, and that way is by practicing and writing about your strategies repeatedly.

Are you ready with your notebook and all set to start? Wait, take a moment to think about your schedule. Take into consideration of how and when you want to work on this material and when you can best fit it into your general routine. To get up to speed with your new learned skills, daily practice is the only way to go. Try to set aside at least a few minutes of your time every day. The primary point is, give a thought to how you will integrate this book into your routine.

To reach longer-term goals of sustained peace of mind and inner calm, consider breaking the material down into small, doable steps so you eventually work through the strategies discussed in the entire book, at the pace that suits your life.

The strategies in this book are simple to carry out. They are all evidence based, meaning research has proven their effectiveness. They come from cognitive behavioural therapy (CBT), acceptance and commitment therapy (ACT, pronounced like the word act), and mindfulness practices.

How To Use This Book

Psychology is a young science, and there is still quite a bit we do not know. However, we do know how to treat anxiety. Most people who consistently use psychological tools in this book will find relief.

Before we begin, I would like to mention that I am not a trained psychologist, nor I promote any medications or drugs that will help you cure anxiety. No medication will ever cure your anxiety, they only help you reduce its effect and get you up to face your day with positivity and overall helps you be yourself. I am writing this book to the best of my knowledge and all the fact or statistics stated are well researched. I advise reader's discretion while you read through the book.

This book contains 8 chapters with an additional at last which is the author's case study. The case study that I have mentioned is typically noted from my live interview with some people who have been facing anxiety symptoms or dealing with it currently. A person's identity is kept confidential, and I add no personal information from the interview in the chapter.

As you read the book, the first chapter will give you an in-depth knowledge of what is anxiety. We will then see 3 levels of anxiety that people face, based on its severity.

Also, from this chapter, we will learn 5 major types of anxiety disorder. We will get to know what anxiety triggers are and how we can identify our anxiety triggers to better understand our feelings with information on how to respond to each different type of triggers while we experience it individually. We know often people get confused between fear and anxiety, so at the end of chapter 1 we will see how fear differs from anxiety and how we can simply understand it.

In chapter 2 we will learn about all the feelings underneath your anxiety and how it is affected. We will see how to better accommodate all the changes to your role in life. We will investigate the physical symptoms that a person may experience in anxiety and how to cope with it. Also, we will see mental symptoms that entail with anxiety disorders. In this chapter we will study various strategies and ways to deal with the mental health issue, there are various tasks and self-exercise that you will need to complete for getting better results. Try to set aside a good amount of time for practicing and completing all tasks given. Go at your own pace, do not rush through this chapter. Try to understand everything that is mentioned and integrate into the routine and try to follow the most out of it. You are bound to see noticeable positive changes in two to four weeks of following it.

Chapter 3 teaches you different yoga positions, also known as asana, that you can try to get relief from anxious thoughts and feelings. I have discussed about 11 yoga asanas with an image of the last position, steps to properly perform, and details about the muscle that will work and affect in your body because of that yoga. Try to spare at least 15 minutes of your day early morning or in the evening after your work to practice these yoga positions. It is fine if you are not able to perform all asanas shown, try to perform a couple of them alternatively every day.

If you do not see a positive outcome even after following the strategies and yoga exercise, you might think of another option and start psychotherapy. Chapter 4 will give you all information relating to therapy sessions. You will know the reasons people opt for going to a therapist. We will then see all the different types of therapy available and how it can help you ease anxiety and its symptoms. We will discuss some points on how you can make most out of the therapy sessions once you decide and go for therapy. It also mentions some common reasons that people make to avoid therapy sitting in the chapter. I have then tried to point out some myths that produce stigma in people and countered it with the equivalent fact to stop its spread.

Food has a major impact on your mood. The kind of food you eat brings out a big difference in your behavior and thinking. Chapter 5 mainly focuses on some healthy diets you will probably add to your diet post reading it. I mention proper scientific reasoning and it's nutrient that help you feel at ease from anxiety for your information in this chapter. Try to add as many foods as you can in your diet and observe the difference. Take care of any allergy you might have regarding any food product and try to eliminate that food from the list. If you have any doubts, consult your doctor before you make your first move in this.

Keep medication as the last resort. No medication can cure anxiety, they can only reduce your feelings caused by anxiety by some chemical compounds and their effect on your brain. Chapter 6 discusses mainly four major medication the doctor prescribes that that will help you manage your anxiety so you can function best and carry on with your day-to-day routine. Try not getting addicted to these medications and always consult your doctor before taking them. I do not promote or sell any kinds of products that are mentioned in this chapter.

If numbers and maths do not interest you, then you can skip chapter 7, as it gives real-world statistics and insights on data relating to anxiety in the world. Being a maths student myself, I could not resist myself from adding relevant information and data in the form of this chapter. I would still suggest you read it once. It is for information purposes only and does not have to do anything with your feelings and strategies coping with anxiety. All the data shown are real and result from research carried out in 2017.

Last, Chapter 8 will teach you so many new things and is also the summary chapter that will help you stay in course after you have finished reading this book. This chapter introduces you to another concept of building your support network and taking time to connect with all that matters to you. It will also help you identify your team that you can call for help, be it late in the night or Sunday afternoon, they will always stand by your side to support you in everything you are facing. This chapter will also make you understand the benefits of the support group and show you ways how to find one near your locality or town. If there are no support groups nearby, you can also start one of your own, you will learn some tips if you opt to start your support group from this chapter.

As discussed, I have added some case studies at the very end of the book. These are notes from a confidential interview with some people who experienced anxiety disorders in the past or are facing it.

I hope this book serves its purpose to help you alleviate anxiety and make peace with yourself. Try to perform and carry out as many strategies as you could. Follow them in your daily routine. Always believe in yourself and the sky is the limit. Give it time, everything will be better once again.

1. Let Us Take A Deep Dive

1. Let Us Take A Deep Dive

Since ages now people have been giving multiple definitions to anxiety, some of them are easily relatable whereas some are too scientific to understand. The medical definition of Anxiety states - "A feeling of apprehension and fear, characterized by physical symptoms such as palpitations, sweating, and feelings of stress".

Anxiety congruences with fear, but when a person terrorizes in fear, they know what they are frightened of - whereas anxiety is often less specific. We discuss differentiation between fear and anxiety in the latter part of the chapter.

Different flavors of anxiety, a person experiencing anxiety would fall under one of the below-discussed levels of anxiety.

1. Mild anxiety

If you think or wonder, you are alone dealing with all the hassle and there is no one to understand you. You might as well be wrong about it. Every person living by default falls under this category. Mild anxiety is the most common category, and all of us experience it on a day-to-day basis. Some under certain situations, whereas some during most situations. While you experience it, you may feel uneasy in your stomach, or you may notice a slight increase in your pulse while sitting idle. But believe me anxiety at this level can also be beneficial, it helps you to focus, increase alertness, and keeps you aware of your surroundings.

2. Moderate anxiety

Quite like that what you read in mild anxiety but with time can become more severe and overwhelming, you may feel more nervous, agitated, and disquiet. You find yourself worrying and concentrated on the one thing, event, or situation that is making you feel anxious and you will disregard everything that is taking place around you. That is where you might start to experience stronger physical and emotional anxiety symptoms such as muscle tension, trembling voice, pain in your back, sweaty palms, and often you may notice changes in your sleeping pattern. Emotionally, you may be invested in feeling more sensitive to minor topics than normal, and you may also feel less confident.

3. Severe anxiety

At the highest level, you stop to think rationally and often end up experiencing severe panic. All-day you might feel afraid and confused, disquieted, withdrawn, and agitated. You may also find it very difficult to think straight.

During the night while sleeping your breathing may quicken and you perspire while your muscles will feel very tense.

Now with that knowledge let us try to understand the five major types of anxiety disorders. Many people with anxiety may experience over one type of anxiety condition. If you relate to having over one type of anxiety than do not feel worried, you are not alone.

1. Generalized Anxiety Disorder (GAD)

You may feel anxious about most of the days, worrying about a variety of small things taking place around you. You may also worry about random imaginary events that have not occurred yet. This anxiety disorder is characterized by chronic anxiety, excessive worry, and tension. Most of the time, you feel anxious even when there is nothing to provoke it.

2. Obsessive-Compulsive Disorder (OCD)

You find yourself repeating a pattern of action repeatedly. Actions may include hand washing, checking, counting, or cleaning. We often perform them repeatedly, hoping to prevent obsessive thoughts or to make them go away. This anxiety disorder is characterized by recurrent, unwanted thoughts or repetitive behaviours, also known as obsession or compulsions. While you perform these so-called "rituals," however, it gives you only temporary solace, and not performing them markedly makes you more anxious.

3. Post-Traumatic Stress Disorder (PTSD)

You feel traumatized over a terrifying event that has occurred to you. You feel threatened by it. Some traumatic events that trigger this disorder include violent personal assaults, accidents, natural or human-caused disasters, or military combat.

4. Panic Disorder

You feel sudden terror even when there is no real danger. You start to feel as if you are losing all your control. This anxiety disorder and is characterized by unforeseen and repeated episodes of potent fear accompanied by physical symptoms that may include an increase in pulse, chest or stomach pain, weakness, difficulties in breathing, tingly or numb hands, or sweaty palms. Panic attacks can happen anytime, anywhere, and with no forewarning.

5. Social Anxiety Disorder

You may find everyday interaction makes you feel anxious about self-consciousness and embarrassment because you fear being scrutinized or judged by others. This anxiety disorder characterized by overwhelming anxiety and excessive self-consciousness in common social situations. Your anxiety may be limited to an only single type of situation – fear of speaking in formal or informal topics, or sometimes drinking or eating when surrounded by people around – or, in its worse form, may be so broad that you might experience symptoms mostly when around other known or unknown people at social gatherings or family functions.

What are Anxiety Triggers and How to identify them?

Statistically, according to the Anxiety and Depression Association of America, anxiety disorders are incredibly common, and they touch an estimated 40 million people in the United States. Also, according to the 2017 survey by Indian Health Institutions, it was known that 45 million people are suffering from various mental disorders accounting for 3.46% of the total population in India. So, what exactly causes these anxieties and anxiety disorders can be quite confusing and complicated. The majority of the time is it likely to be a combination of multiple factors, inclusive of genetics and environmental reasons play a vital role. However, it is clear from a medical perspective that some events, feeling, experiences, and emotions that you hold on to may cause symptoms of anxiety to begin at a small stage or may have a long-time effect. These above-mentioned elements that make you anxious, frightened, and apprehensive are called triggers.

Before we begin to know these triggers, we must know anxiety triggers can vary from person-to-person, but many triggers are common to experience by most people. You may even find while reading that you have multiple triggers, that is true, but do not worry. Also, anxiety attacks can be triggered for no reason at all. That is why identifying them is a very important step in managing them.

With that in hand, let us know some of the anxiety triggers and later see some tips that can help you find out which trigger aligns with your anxiety.

1. Caffeine

Are you one of those many people who rely on their morning cup of joe to wake up, or to carry out any other task? It might trigger or worsen anxiety. Mostly it is noticed that people with panic disorder and social anxiety disorder are very sensitive to the anxiety induced effects of caffeine.

Respond – Simply work on cutting back your caffeine intake by switching to non-caffeinated options whenever possible.

2. Health issues

Are you recently diagnosed with a severe illness or chronic medical condition? That can be deeply upsetting and worrying, they may trigger anxiety or make it worse. This type of trigger is powerful because of the immediate and personal feelings it produces within you. There may also be sudden changes taking place in your body that are adjusting to certain situations.

Respond–Be proactive, engage more often with your doctor. Talking with your therapist may also be useful. Also, in the latter part of the book, we will see different approaches to overcome these types of situations.

3. Medications

Are you consuming more than the regular amount of certain prescription and over-the-counter medications? They may trigger symptoms of anxiety as well. Active ingredients in the composition of these medications sometimes make you feel uneasy or unwell. These feelings can set off a chain reaction of events in your mind and body that eventually leads to an increase in symptoms of anxiety. Some common medications that may trigger anxiety are cough and congestion medications, birth control pills, also weight loss medications, and many more.

Respond – Have a talk with your doctor about your condition and that you are consuming these medications, how these drugs make you feel, and look for an alternative option that does not trigger your anxiety or worsen your symptoms.

4. Negative thinking

Have you heard the quote, "Once you control your mind, you can conquer your body", it is true, your mind controls much of your body, and that is a hundred percent true with the anxiety as well. If you feel frustrated, the words you say to yourself and others can trigger greater feelings of anxiety.

Respond – Refocus on your language and feelings if you tend to use a lot of negative words while you think about yourself and others close to you.

5. Skipping meals

Are you skipping your meal more often or have a feeling to have a loss in appetite? When you do not eat, your level of sugar in the blood may drop, which leads to jittery hands and a rumbling tummy. Also, it possesses a threat to anxiety. Eating a well-balanced meal will help you live a well-balanced life.

Respond – Eat healthy snacks more often when you find it difficult to have three meals a day, it will help you prevent low blood sugar, feelings of nervousness, and agitation.

6. Financial difficulty

Are you living under heavy debt, or without a job, or having a very low income and finding it difficult to hold everything in place? Unanticipated bills or money crunch can trigger your anxiety too. Even before the global coronavirus pandemic and resulting economic fallout, an American Psychological Association (APA) study found that 72% of Americans feel stressed about money at least some time. The recent economic difficulties mean that even more of us are now facing financial struggles and hardship.

Respond – Seek professional help, if you have experienced parents or adults at home, talk to them regarding the situation. Talk to a financial advisor. The feeling of having a companion and a guide who can talk through the process may ease your concern.

7. Conflict

Did you recently break up with your love interest? Arguments, disagreements, relationship problems, these sensitive issues can trigger anxiety. If you tend to have conflict triggers, then most of the time you will not be willing to get into a fight with anyone about anything.

You may also find yourself skipping healthy discussions and play safe not to talk about it. Scuttling away like an alarmed crab every time somebody seems intent on disagreement is not productive, and it can hobble your professional and emotional progress.

Respond – You will need to learn and incorporate some conflict resolution strategies in your life. You can start with simple, not to react to all situations aggressively, rather respond to it with a composed mind.

8. Social events or family gatherings

Do you find difficulties in being in a room full of people, or experience anxiety before the actual event? You are not alone. Smallest of events that require having small talk or interact with people around to the largest of events such as giving a speech or performance or attending an interview can trigger feelings of anxiety. It is obvious during these situations for a person to feel a little anxious and nervous. Sometimes, however, the anxiety is so intense that it stops you from engaging in activities that others would otherwise enjoy. You start to feel excessively self-conscious and become socially withdrawn.

Respond – Whenever you have a social gathering to attend to, always bring along a companion with whom you feel comfortable. Also, work it out with your advisor to make these events more manageable in the long term.

Also, positive reinforcement from friends and colleagues can help you feel more comfortable and confident in yourself.

9. Stress

Ever feel anxious when you do not complete your work assignments, or you are stuck in traffic jams, or you miss your daily subway to reach your work? These are day-to-day stressors that will make any human being anxious. But long-term or chronic stress can often lead to anxiety or make it worse. Excessive stress can also lead to behavioural changes that we will discuss further in this book like skipping meals, drinking alcohol, or not getting enough sleep. These factors can trigger anxiety.

Respond–A therapist or counselor can help you learn to recognize your sources of stress and handle them when they become overwhelming or problematic. Some coping mechanisms will be discussed and acknowledge in the latter part of this book.

10. Personal triggers

Have you ever felt that smell, or a place, even a song, or some talks make you feel anxious? Personal triggers either consciously or unconsciously remind you of terrible memory or traumatic event in your life. Individuals with post-traumatic stress disorder (PTSD) frequently experience anxiety triggers from environmental triggers.

Respond – As these triggers are the most difficult to identify, but a mental health specialist is trained to help you identify them with ease. You may meet one specialist and talk to them about your feelings. Identifying personal triggers may take a long time, but it is important so you can learn to overcome them with professional help.

You are in a friendly, normal conversation with another person right in front of you. Everything is going well as it should until – BANG! There is a sudden increase in your blood pressure, you are hyperventilating, and you build a distinct urge from within to strangle the other person.

Even when the person in front of you made an impassive comment, you still find yourself to avert yourself from screaming down their throat and gouging out their eyes.

Then you must wonder what happened?

You got triggered – that is what just happened.

Cogitating on the situation later, you might end up realizing how disproportionate your rage was, and how uncomfortable you sounded. If you feel you are the kind of person who feels like a matchstick just waiting to be ignited by anyone around, you might have a problem with your anxiety triggers. It is very much important to identify it and take control of it.

If you succeed in identifying your triggers, then you can easily workaround to avoid them and to cope with them. You can learn specific coping strategies to handle the triggers when they happen. Let us now understand how to identify triggers.

There are three simple tips that you will need to practice in identifying your triggers.

First, start a journal. Just the same as a personal diary. Write whenever your anxiety is noticeable and record in your own words what you think might have led to the trigger. There are various mobile applications available in the application store that can help you track your anxiety.

Second, work with a therapist. Sometimes anxiety triggers can be very difficult to identify, but a mental health specialist is trained to identify and rectify similar situations, they can help you identify your triggers. Some methods they use to in the process are talk therapy, journaling, or various methods.

Finally, Be honest with yourself. You may start to notice that anxiety causes negative thoughts and lack of self-assessments, but if you let them come in between that will make identifying triggers difficult mainly because of your anxious reactions. Try to be as patient as you can with yourself and be willing to explore things in your past to identify how they are still in your head and understand how you may be still affected by it today.

Let us now try to understand the major difference between fear and anxiety. As mentioned before at the start of the chapter, anxiety congruences with fear, but we know they are not the same. To understand it is a very basic and simple term, take a minute and interpret the image shown below.

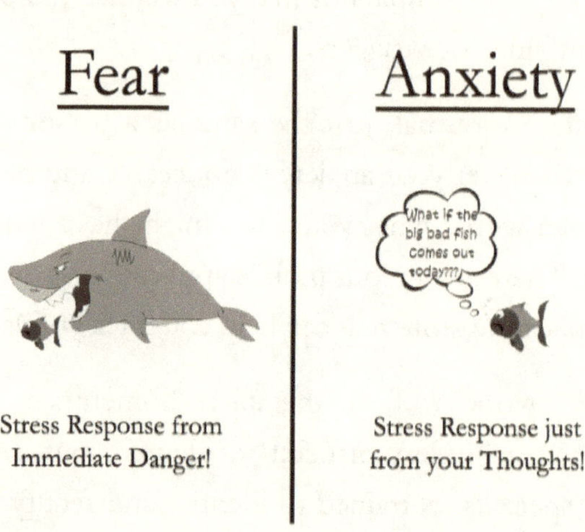

Fear is what we have known from the origin, if not known we can still figure it out, but anxiety, it is unknown and vague. It cannot be known easily. Fear on one hand is definite, we know it will be passed once we ignore and stop doing what frightens us, but anxiety, it is indefinite; we do not know when it will end or when we will be able to overcome it. Fear is what starts from the external sources whereas anxiety starts internally from within us.

Fear is what we have in front of us, here and now, but anxiety, we have no clue; it is just like a thought. An event might have happened, or just some future assumption that makes us worry. Fear shows a strong association with the fight-or-flight response, but on the other hand, anxiety is weakly associated with the fight-or-flight response. Fear is always non-conflictual whereas anxiety is always conflictual.

Takeaways

- Anxiety responds to treatment. You can and will get better.
- Knowing the type of anxiety disorder will help you cope with it.
- Having to relate to over one anxiety trigger is common. You are not alone.
- If you identify your triggers, then you can easily workaround to avoid them and to cope with them.
- Fear does congruence with anxiety, but they are not the same.

2. It Is Inevitable

2. It Is Inevitable

You tend to gain greater emotional control, as you learn to better identify your feelings. As a result, you will be less affected by intense emotional reactions, such as emotional meltdowns, panic attacks, crying spells, and worried thinking. Also, once you know how and what you are feeling, you will be better off at addressing the genuine issue in hand and feel a lot better. Some deeper feelings that may be underneath your anxiety are,

Anger - Anger cues the body to self-protect through physical force, self-assertion, or boundary setting.

Anxiety - Anxiety triggers adrenaline, which puts the body into high alert, primed for action, and protection.

Guilty - Guilt keeps people in line with societal laws and norms designed for protecting people.

Love - Love bonds couples, children, families, and tribes. It is the glue that connects people.

Pleasure - Pleasure is a tonic for negative emotions and motivates us to do certain things to experience more pleasure.

Sadness - Sadness is protective because it allows the self to mark time while grief and problem-solving can take place.

Shame - Shame signifies social status in a group and keeps people under group expectations.

The above reference is taken from the book "be calm." By Jill P. Weber, 2019.

Accommodating changes to your role in life.

You may also have noticed, when you were ready to accept and planned to face life changes, still you find it difficult to adjust than your expectation. Major changes in your role, like becoming a parent, losing the one you cared about the most or retiring, usually affect the very important area of your life, such areas include,

Your house, where you live.

Your thoughts, how you define yourself.

Your ambitions, the goal that you set in life.

Your image, people's expectation of you.

Your beliefs, something you greatly look forward to.

Your friends, who you have around to support you.

Sometimes not directly, but the difficulty, challenges, and conflict that aligns with these life alteration events can contribute to anxiety.

Always remember one thing. Any major change for one person can affect the entire family, not only for one person. For example, when a new baby is born in a family it involves not only new roles and responsibilities for the parents, but rather it brings changes for the entire family. You might have noticed yourself. These changes require some amount of effort and change by everyone in the family.

Physical Symptoms

Do you think just like everyone else; anxiety only messes up with your thought process and your emotional effects? That is not at all true. Physical symptoms of anxiety do not get as much attention as the mental symptom, but the reality is anxiety can wreak just as much havoc on the body physically as it can on the mind mentally. Mona Potter, M.D., medical director at McLean Anxiety Mastery Program in Boston says, "From head to toe, almost every system can be affected just by nature of your body releasing a lot of stress hormones".

When you are anxious, though, your fear and worry are the threat, prompting your sympathetic nervous system, which controls involuntary processes like your breathing and heart rate, to kick into top gear. This leads your adrenal glands to release hormones such as adrenaline and cortisol, according to the Mayo Clinic. This domino effect is behind anxiety's physical symptoms.

"When a person experiences anxiety, it's essentially the fight-or-flight system kicking in and saying, 'Danger!'" Neda Gould, Ph.D., a clinical psychologist and associate director of the Johns Hopkins Bayview Anxiety Disorders Clinic.

That makes it very important for us to concede these physical symptoms that are happening to you and your body because if you do not, it is very difficult to seek out for a treatment that you need to feel better. So, let us now try to understand some of the biggest physical symptoms of anxiety.

1. A sudden increase in your heart rate

One of the classic signs of anxiety that is faced by most of the people, according to the National Institute of Mental Health (NIMH). In medical terms, when you are dealing with something very stressful and your adrenal glands churn out hormones like adrenaline and cortisol, receptors in your heart react by speeding up your heartbeat. This in turn enables you to pump more blood to your big muscles so you could theoretically flee or combat a threat. But if you are dealing with anxiety, the racing heart can often make you feel even more nervous in a vicious cycle.

2. Shortening of breath

Our brain is wired to react to fearful situations with the fight-or-flight response. So, when you feel anxious your body response boosts how quickly you are sending blood around your body, with that your breathing might increase to provide you with more oxygen.

If you are breathing too quickly, as known as hyperventilation, you could intensify a lot of the physical anxiety symptoms on the list because of your oxygen-carbon dioxide balance get out of proportion, according to the U.S. National Library of Medicine.

3. Exhausted too frequently

The post-anxiety crash is yet another symptom that is observed most times. The primary reason has to do with the crash that you feel after your adrenaline runs out. This phenomenon is called adrenal fatigue. Anxiety always keeps you vigilant. Your body is constantly preparing you to fight or to fee; and so, your body is always flooded with energy and you feel spry all the time to respond to a threat. Then, when that adrenaline runs its course, your body experiences crash that can leave you feeling drained and exhausted.

4. Sleeping issues

First, it is not just that anxiety contributes to sleeping problems. Sleep issues like insomnia can make you prone to anxiety too.

A person with anxiety might have a tough time falling asleep and/or staying asleep, or might have restless and unsatisfying sleep, according to the NIMH. Because of the high level of hormones, like cortisol and adrenaline, make it hard to get proper sleep during the night. Also, the racing thoughts that can come with anxiety are not friendly for a great sleep.

5. Muscle tension and pain

It is observed that many people with anxiety report feeling tight in their back, neck, or shoulders. Your muscles tense up as part of your stress response. Holding on to the tense muscle so rigid for a longer period during the day can lead to pain. When you clench your jaw or feel muscle tension all the way up in your head, you may even experience severe to minor headaches.

6. The stomach is messed up

Researchers have identified a powerful connection between the gut and the brain. Like the brain, the gut is full of nerves. It contains the largest area of nerves outside the brain, with the digestive tract and the brain sharing many of the same nerve connections. May it be a simple thing or a chronic event that is making you anxious, but it can have a deep impact on your digestive system. When you are anxious, your body secretes various hormones and chemicals in your digestive tract, where they interfere with the digestion process. They tend to have a negative effect on your gut, and it decreases antibody production. This chemical imbalance may cause various gastrointestinal conditions. There is also the fact that anxiety-induced lifestyle choices like eating foods that do not agree with you or not exercising can affect your digestion as well.

7. Excessive sweat

We have a love/hate relationship with sweat. Our body's sweating mechanism is a marvel of physiological engineering. When triggered by the hypothalamus in the brain, apocrine and eccrine sweat glands secrete sweat. The evaporation of sweat, composed mostly of water, salt, and electrolytes, creates a cooling effect that helps maintain body temperature. Sweating at the gym or when working out is desirable and keeps us healthy. So, it gets us to thinking when does our sweat turn from desirable to deplorable? When your sympathetic nervous system gets activated, it can influence the sweat glands all over your body.

Nervous sweating often leads to even more sweating- sometimes even out of our control because we start to feel self-conscious when surrounded by people.

8. Feeling shaky

As your body prepares to deal with the stressor, after interpreting the anxiousness as a signal that you will be in a need to stand your ground to fight or escape from danger. Your muscles become ready to act, leading to a trembling sensation, twitching, or shaking. These tremors caused by anxiety are called psychogenic tremors.

9. Easily startled

You start to notice that you jump or are startled at even the smallest of things, insignificant sounds, or noises, which normally would not gain your attention even. You feel that you are usually jumpy, nervous, and jittery. Constantly being on guard has been linked with an increased "startle response," which could be why you practically jump out of your shoes if someone taps you on the shoulder on an anxious day.

10. Hard time swallowing

You start to feel a tightness in your throat or even feel like something is stuck in your throat. This feeling or sensation is called globus sensation, and it is completely unrelated to eating. Although the exact reasoning is not yet clear, but it can make anxiety even worse.

Mental Symptoms

Two parts of the brain are thought to be key players in the production and processing of anxiety – the amygdala and the hippocampus.

"The amygdala is an almond-shaped structure deep in the brain that is believed to be a communications hub between the parts of the brain that process incoming sensory signals and the parts that interpret these signals. It can alert the rest of the brain that a threat is present and trigger a fear or anxiety response.

The emotional memories stored in the central part of the amygdala may play a role in anxiety disorders involving very distinct fears, such as fears of dogs, spiders, or flying. The hippocampus is the part of the brain that encodes threatening events into memories."
(National Institute of Mental Health).

Once your brain has encountered any threat, may it be actual or perceived, it will release a surge of chemicals, like cortisol and norepinephrine. These chemicals will give you a natural boost in reflex time, speed, and perception. They in turn cause our heart to pump faster than normal to get more blood and oxygen circulating through your bodies. In simple terms, you go into "survival mode."

Some mental effects and feelings that are common to have while you are facing anxiety are hereby listed below. If you feel you are experiencing them, do not worry, it is common to feel while you are dealing with your anxiety.

1. You feel tense, nervous, and are unable to relax most of the time.

2. You always have a sense of dread or continuous fear of the worst.

3. You feel like the entire world around you is speeding up whereas you are slowing down.

4. You constantly feel that other people can notice you are anxious, and you are just looking at you.

5. You keep on thinking and cannot stop worrying, or even feel that something bad will happen if you stop worrying.

6. You think and worry about the worst, that is the anxiety itself, and keep wondering if it might happen again.

7. You seek a lot of reassurance from the surrounding people, or you might as well think those people close to you are angry and upset with you.

8. You think that you are on the verge of losing touch with reality.

9. You keep on ruminating, thinking about the unsatisfactory experiences, or situations you faced repeatedly.

10. You start to depersonalize; you start to feel disconnected from your mind and body.

Strategies to deal with anxiety

1. Choose 3 words of intent + affirmation

Let us now do a small exercise, it will make your engagement and trust me you are about to make some genuine progress now. Choose any 3 words that are both affirmation and intentional for yourself that you would like to say out every night before going to sleep and every morning while waking up.

You may even want to set your personal device wallpaper to these words, or record it and set it as your morning alarm tone, you may even go old school and write it down on a piece of paper and stick it to your mirror.

Confused? What to choose. I will give you an example of three words that I have chosen for myself.

I am Attentive; I am Assertive; I am Alive.

It will be interesting to know what 3 words you come up with. How will you be using these 3 words? These 3 words that you will choose will help you and show you how you will act when around other people. It will show you a sense of ownership of yourself. These words will guide you in ways you want to be internally and externally with people around and allow you to empower yourself into being the best version of yourself. It will help you to stay on course and will give you enormous power to your mind as you have chosen the words yourself and that is exactly what you want. The feeling of anxiety will find it hard to creep in when you are intentional and affirmative throughout the day.

Are you ready now? Take time, think, and then write your three words in the space below.

I am __________________________.

I am __________________________.

I am __________________________.

2. Write

Write your heart out. Write whatever comes to your mind. Verbal vomit it all out! Yes, you heard it right, try asking questions to your mind like why you felt the way you did, or behave and write your answers. Manage a personal diary or be techno-savvy and record all your answers in an audio diary on your personal device. If you dislike writing much, still try once. Writing is a powerful tool and trust me. It will help you. When you write, you will feel as if all the negative weights have been lifted off from your shoulders. You tend to feel lighter. Another positive side of writing is, it is accounted for, next time you need answers to your why(s), open your diary and read it through. It will help you reassess your situation.

3. Be curious

Ask questions to your self, being curious about your feelings and wanting to know why behind why you are feeling what you are feeling as you are feeling is a form of self-analysis and not judging. The best thing about being curious is, it will help you to shift your focus and attention to something else rather than thinking about anxiety itself. Try to see minute details in your feelings with loving-kindness and do not think that you are being judgemental about yourself.

Yippee! Its time for a new exercise. Given in the space below, try to write three questions about yourself or your feeling that you do not have answers to. Simple. Just write it down.

Q1.

____

____

____

Q2.

____

____

____

Q3.

____

____

____

Now continue to read the book further. Are you curious now what will happen to your questions? Good to know that you are curious. After reading and applying lessons in the book, try to revisit these sets of questions and see if you get your answers to it.

4. Be in present

Often worrying about the future takes away the magnificence of the present moment that is right in front of you. You can not and never will be able to live somewhere that has not happened yet. The present is your gift. Unwrap it. Wallow in it. Heed it. Be happy about it.

You may wonder how you can be in the present? For this, you will need to continuously keep a check and ask yourself if you are currently freaking out about something in the past or the future. Most of the time it happens you are physically present in the moment but mentally you are somewhere else. Notice things around you and understand that these are the only situation currently in your control, nothing else. You may want to set up a reminder pop up every hour or two on your personal device that will prompt you with questions like, "Are you being in present right now?" or "Where are your thoughts right now?". Try to spare at least a minute when this notification comes on your device and try to get back to the present if you are not. In your personal diary keep track of the count, the number of times you were not being in the present when the notification popped up. It would be great to see the number going down as days progress. At first, you may feel it tiring to manage with so much such, but over time these all may come as natural.

5. Be self-aware

The more self-aware you are when anxiety strikes, the better it will help you in the process of identifying your trigger, as we discussed in our prior chapter. The majority of the time it happens with people that they do not even know why they are anxious! Well, to be honest, how can you expect to be fighting it if you do not know what is causing it. Getting to the root cause of any matter helps you remove the problem once in for all anxiety is no different. Be more self-aware when you are feeling anxious or worrying about an event or situation. Notice what just happened right before those sensations. Write it down in your diary or record it on your personal device. It will allow you to think in a different direction right at that moment while you are figuring the root cause, you are not thinking about your anxious feeling rather you are introspecting, following the problem-solving approach.

6. Worry timer

This is an actual strategy used by psychologists in their day-to-day therapy classes. It is a tried and tested method, also it is liked by most anxiety patients. Next time when you have anxiety or you feel you are worrying a lot over a matter, set a timer for around 10-20 minutes on your personal device, that is your "worry time". As crazy as it sounds, but it is true. In your worry time, you may feel whatever you want to feel, worry as much as you want, be anxious about anything, let it all out. Do all that you want to or feel like doing. Once your worry time is up, go back to your day. Why? As I mentioned as crazy as it sounds but think of a situation when you get stuck into an infinite hole of worries that in most cases can take away your entire day, week, or even months. Instead of turning your 1 hour into 2, then 4, then 6, and then 8, better just set a timer for about 1 hour, if you think you have too much to worry too and then once done, get back to your day and start working with your daily routine. This is not at all to suppress what you are feeling, instead, this is to let it out healthily and naturally.

So next time when you think you need time to worry and shout out loud, do not worry, set a timer and get done with your stuff, once the timer goes off, it's time for you to shut the door for that thoughts and re-join with your normal tasks. This method is ancient and since ages, many famous people have been following it in their daily routine. It gives a limit to yourself and keeps you in discipline to follow through on those limits.

Try it next time and see how it changes you!

7. Step outside

Every one of us has a couple of places around our home or in the town where we like to sit and be us. Some of you might be reading this book in one of your places. If you think you are a person who does not like to step outside of the house much and do not have those spaces that I am talking about, do not worry, it's time for you to step outside now and search for those great places. It is not too difficult, those places might be the outer stairs of your house or swing that is placed in your clubhouse, even the empty chair on security cabin works. If you already have those places simply write below in the space provided, if not take a week or two to search for those places and then write it down.

1. ____.

2. ____.

3. ____.

While you are sitting there, observe things around, notice little things. Just plug in your earphones, stare at the sky and enjoy the soothing breeze and nature around. Whatever it may be, but getting outside to breathe some fresh air does wonders.

8. Do what you love

No one is as busy as they could not even spare 10 minutes of their day in doing one thing that they love. Painting is your passion, then be it. Whatever you love, music, gym, photography, playing an instrument, literature, reading, do more of it and try to incorporate more of these into your daily life. Feeling too lazy to do something, no problem just watch a comedy movie, something that will make you laugh, or tune into your favourite radio, these will help you distract from anxiety too. Distraction may indeed give you a quick relief, but it is a band-aid solution and not a permanent fix. You can not make a habit of getting distracted away from anxiety for a longer period, but if it is helping you in the short run, then do not worry, just go for it.

List three things below that you love and plan on doing next time when you feel anxious.

1. _______________________________________.

2. _______________________________________.

3. _______________________________________.

9. It is impermanent

Nothing has ever remained consistent in this world, never it will ever. Just like everything has passed, this shall pass too. You yourself have experienced it, even you are anxious it has not stayed with you forever, continuously. Neither will it this time as well. I know how frustrating it feels when people around tell you that what you are feeling is hypothetical and it is never going to happen in reality, it is something that you are just feeling and shut it up and calm down. I am not trying to refute your feelings. What you are feeling is real for you, in your headspace that is something happening to you at this moment. What I am trying to say is, when you feel anxious over a feeling, try to reframe the thought from different angles, try to build a different framework, your perspective will make a tremendous difference in your thought process and your feeling.

10. Meditation

You may wonder that meditation is a magic elixir that will make anxiety go away from your life forever. That is not at all true. Meditation will help you incredibly to get more focus in your life, it will help you to bring in peace, it will make you calm and composed, but having this misconception that meditation heals anxiety is not right. It will help you enormously. You should make a habit of meditating every morning, which will bring in a big positive change in your life. Through meditation, you will familiarize yourself with anxiety-inducing thoughts. You learn to see them, sit with them, and let them go. In doing so, you will learn two important things: thoughts do not define you, and thoughts are not real. Within this newfound perspective, you will be able to evanesce your relationship with anxiety, differentiating between what is an irrational feeling and what is true.

You can engage yourself in meditation with the help of various personal device applications, also by seeing through online videos. Meditation is so easy, once you have the proper grip of it, you can even do it in between your meetings while at work or in your bed before you go to sleep. There is a complete chapter in the latter part of the book that will discuss different yoga posture that could help you with anxiety.

Takeaways

- You will gain better control over yourself once you identify your feelings.
- A major change in the role may trigger anxiety, accept it, and try to adjust to it.
- Anxiety is not only about mental stress but also look for physical symptoms that are associated with it.
- We discussed 10 strategies that will help you alleviate anxiety, try to work on them.

- Nothing is permanent, these feelings shall pass too.

3. A FOR A

3. A For A

A for A means, "Asana" meaning different postures in yoga for "Anxiety".

You may as well want to turn to yoga when feelings of anxiety start to creep in. You may find that focusing on both your breath and your ability to be present in each pose can help quiet negative mental chatter and boost your overall mood. You may not be able to perform all 11 yoga postures that are discussed further in this chapter but try to practice at least two posture a day. Learn all of them alternatively and when you find time at weekends, try to perform them more often.

To get the most out of your session while performing, please take note of the feelings that move throughout your body as you come into each pose. Allow yourself to feel and experience whatever emotions arise in your mind.

If you feel your thoughts start to scatter, do not worry, gently bring your mind back to the yoga mat and continue with your practice.

Below are the 11 yoga postures that will help you alleviate anxiety. I take this list from a blog post on © Healthline Media, a Red Ventures Company.

1. Hero pose (Virasana)

This seated posture can help you find your center. Focusing on your breath may help you find ease in the stillness of this pose.

Muscles worked:

- erector spinae
- quadriceps
- knee muscles
- ankle muscles

To do this:

- Get into a kneeling position. Your knees should be together, and your feet should be slightly wider than your hips.
- Keep the tops of your feet flat on the floor.

- If this is uncomfortable, put a cushion or block under your buttocks, thighs, or calves.
- Place your hands on your thighs.
- Sit up straight to open your chest and lengthen your spine.
- Hold this pose for up to 5 minutes.

2. Tree pose (Vriksasana)

This classic standing pose may help you focus inward, quieting racing thoughts.

Muscles worked:

- abdominals
- psoas
- quadriceps
- tibialis anterior

To do this:

- From standing, bear your weight with your right foot and slowly lift your right foot off the ground.
- Slowly turn the sole of your left foot toward the inside of your left leg.
- Place it on the outside of your left ankle, calf, or thigh.
- Avoid pressing your foot into your knee.
- Bring your hands into any comfortable position. This could be in prayer position in front of your heart or hanging alongside your sides.
- Hold this pose for up to 2 minutes.
- Repeat on the opposite side.

3. Triangle pose (Trikonasana)

This energizing pose can help ease tension in your neck and back.

58

Muscles worked:

- latissimus dorsi
- internal oblique
- gluteus maximus and medius
- hamstrings
- quadriceps

To do this:

- Come into a standing position with your feet wider than your hips.
- Face your left toes forward and your right toes in at a slight angle.
- Lift your arms to extend out from your shoulders. Your palms should face down.
- Extend your torso forward as you reach forward with your left hand.
- Hinge at your hip joint to bring your right hip back. Take your left hand to your leg, the floor, or a block.
- Extend your right arm up toward the ceiling.
- Gaze in any comfortable direction.
- Hold this pose for up to 1 minute.
- Then do the opposite side.

4. Standing forward bend (Uttanasana)

This resting standing pose may help relax your mind while releasing tension in your body.

Muscles worked:

- spinal muscles
- piriformis
- hamstrings
- gastrocnemius
- gracilis

To do this:

- Stand with your feet about hip-width apart and your hands on your hips.
- Exhale as you hinge at the hips to fold forward, keeping a slight bend in your knees.
- Drop your hands to the floor or rest them on a block.
- Tuck your chin into your chest.

- Release tension in your lower back and hips. Your head and neck should hang heavy toward the floor.

- Hold this pose for up to one minute.

5. Fish pose (Matsyasana)

This backbend can help relieve tightness in your chest and back.

Muscles worked:

- intercostals
- hip flexors
- trapezius
- abdominals

To do this:

- Sit with your legs stretched out in front of you.
- Place your hands underneath your buttocks with your palms facing down.
- Squeeze your elbows together and expand your chest.

- Then lean back onto your forearms and elbows, pressing into your arms to stay lifted in your chest.

- If it's comfortable, you may let your head hang back toward the floor or rest it on a block or cushion.

- Hold this pose for up to one minute.

6. Extended puppy pose (Uttana Shishosana)

This heart-opening pose stretches and lengthens the spine to relieve tension.

Muscles worked:

- deltoids
- trapezius
- erector spinae
- triceps

To do this:

- Come into a tabletop position.
- Extend your hands forward a few inches and sink your buttocks down toward your heels.

- Press into your hands and engage your arms muscles, keeping your elbows lifted.
- Gently rest your forehead on the floor.
- Allow your chest to open and soften during this pose.
- Hold this pose for up to two minutes.

7. Child's pose (Balasana)

This relaxing pose may help ease stress and fatigue.

Muscles worked:

- gluteus maximus
- rotator muscles
- hamstrings
- spinal extensors

To do this:

- From a kneeling position, sink back onto your heels.
- Fold forward, walking your hands out in front of you.
- Allow your torso to fall heavy into your thighs, and rest your forehead on the floor.

- Keep your arms extended forward or rest them alongside your body.

- Hold this pose for up to 5 minutes.

8. Head-to-knee forward bend (Janusirsasana)

This pose may help soothe your nervous system.

Muscles worked:

- groin

- hamstrings

- spinal extensors

- gastrocnemius

To do this:

- Sit on the edge of a cushion or folded blanket with your left leg extended.

- Press the sole of your right foot into your left thigh.

- You can place a cushion or block under either knee for support.

- Inhale as you extend your arms overhead.

- Exhale as you hinge at the hips, lengthening your spine to fold forward.
- Rest your hands anywhere on your body or on the floor.
- Hold this pose for up to 5 minutes.
- Then repeat on the opposite side.

9. Seated forward bend (Paschimottanasana)

This pose is thought to calm the mind while relieving anxiety. If you feel that your thoughts have been scattered throughout your practice, take this time to turn inward and come back to your intention.

Muscles worked:

- pelvic muscles
- erector spinae
- gluteus maximus
- gastrocnemius

To do this:

- Sit on the edge of a folded blanket or cushion with your legs straight out in front of you.

- You may keep a slight bend in your knees.
- Inhale to lift up your arms.
- Slowly hinge at your hips to extend forward, resting your hands anywhere on your body or the floor.
- Remain in this pose for up to 5 minutes.

10. Legs-up-the-wall pose (Viparita Karani)

This restorative pose allows for complete relaxation of your mind and body.

Muscles worked:

- hamstrings
- pelvic muscles
- lower back
- front torso
- back of the neck

To do this:

- Sit with your right side against a wall.
- Then lie back as you swing your legs up along the wall.
- Your buttocks should be as close to the wall as is comfortable for you. This could be right up against the wall or a few inches away.
- Relax and soften in your back, chest, and neck. Allow your body to melt into the floor.
- Hold this pose for up to 10 minutes.

11. Reclining bound angle pose
    (Supta Baddha Konasana)

This relaxing pose can help you let go of anxiety while promoting a sense of calmness. You can make it more of a heart opener by placing a block or cushion under your back.

Muscles worked:

- adductors
- groin muscles
- pelvic muscles
- psoas

To do this:

- Lie on your back and bring the soles of your feet together.
- Place cushions under your knees or hips for support.
- Place one hand on your stomach area and one hand on your heart, focusing on your breath.
- Stay in this pose for up to 10 minutes.

Takeaways

- Yoga helps reduces stress and anxiety.
- Perform at least 2 asanas a day to gain better results.

4. Get On The Couch

4. Get On The Couch

A research study conducted by the National Institute of Mental Health found that over half of all patients who received therapy for anxiety, depression, and other mental health conditions experience and succeeded with significant improvement in their symptoms. With this high success rate, it still comes to me with a big surprise that many people still do not seek for therapy because of perceived stigma. While some are afraid of seeming "week" or "broken", where others are just afraid of what therapy may entail.

The truth is, whether you believe it or not, but there are countless benefits to therapy for anxiety and mental health, to state a single, you get to live an improved quality of life. Isn't it enough to get you started?

So, we may wonder why people seek therapy? Since everyone is struggling in different ways, we cannot state a specific reason for it, it varies from case to case, but here are some of the reasons mentioned.

1. Loneliness

That is true, not everyone is gifted with correct life support, or a friend, or family that supports them in what they are feeling. Research shows that majority of the surrounding people cannot understand your struggle and the ones who do are struggling with their life crisis. Not to forget the fact even some symptoms of anxiety may further drive you away from others, which will in turn create a self-perpetuating cycle of loneliness.

2. No control over your thoughts

When your anxious thoughts get out of control, they can affect your ability to work, you might not be able to concentrate in anything you do, maintaining personal relationships may feel like trouble too, that is the correct time you need to build a strong relationship with your therapist.

3. Substance abuse

Most of the people when they do not have anyone to talk to regarding their problems often start to self-medicate themselves with drugs. Drinking excessive alcohol is another problem. These activities will make anxiety conditions worse over time.

You do not have to live with your anxiety your entire life. Treatment can help you overcome it. For most of the anxiety problems, therapy is often the most effective option. That is because unlike anxiety medication, therapy will treat more than just the symptoms of the problem. It mainly focuses on the cause of the problem rather than the problem at the surface itself. Therapy teaches you the tools to overcome anxiety and gives you a clear picture of how to use them.

As none of us would face the same kind of symptoms, or none of us would suffer from some disorder, as the type of anxiety differs completely from person to person, so the therapy should be tailored to your specific symptoms and diagnosis. If you have obsessive-compulsive disorder, for example, then your treatment will differ from someone who is seeking help for post-traumatic stress disorder. With the kind of therapy required, the length of the treatment will also vary from case to case, mainly depends on the severity of your anxiety. We observe the majority of the time it that the therapy treatment tends to be of short tenure. According to the American Psychological Association, many people improve significantly within 8 to 10 therapy sessions.

There are so many different types of therapy used to treat anxiety, we are discussing the major of them in this chapter as well, the leading approaches are cognitive-behavioral therapy (CBT) and exposure therapy. Based on case and severity, each therapy may be used alone, or be advised to use a combination with some other type of therapy. Also, based on the type of therapy, it may be conducted individually or among a group of people experiencing similar anxiety problems. With one common goal at hand – try to alleviate your anxiety, calm your mind, bring peace, and overcome your fear.

1. Cognitive Behavioural Therapy (CBT)

This is the most widely used therapy for anxiety disorders. It is effective in treating social anxiety disorder, generalized anxiety disorder, phobias, and panic disorders.

The beauty of CBT has to do with your thoughts, not your present situation, affects you in how you are feeling and behaving. So, the aim of CBT is to identify and understand your negative thinking and ineffective behavior patterns and interchange them with more realistic thoughts and coping mechanisms.

While you are undergoing your therapy, your therapist acts as a coach teaching you helpful strategies. For instance, think you might do "black-and-white" thinking, where you are assuming everything around and everything happening to you is either all good or all bad. Instead, the therapy will teach you to replace your thoughts with a more realistic approach and change your perception to think that there are many more shades of grey in between. Yes, it takes a while to understand and practice once you start taking the therapy but once you learn and apply, you will be able to manage your fear, worry, and panic.

2. Exposure Therapy

It is the most common type of CBT that is used to treat a variety of anxiety disorders, such as specific phobias, post-traumatic stress disorder, and social anxiety disorder. As the name suggests, this therapy will help you face what you are afraid of.

As you are in session, your therapist will be slowing to introduce you to different anxiety-provoking objects or events. We know this technique as "systematic desensitization", which consists of three steps –

i. Relax – Progressive muscle relaxation, deep breathing, meditation, and guided imagery are some relaxation training methodologies used by the therapist. Your therapist will teach you some above-mentioned techniques to help combat your anxiety.

ii. List – You will be asked to create a list of your anxiety-provoking triggers, in order of intensity according to you.

iii. Expose – In the last step, you will gradually work your way through your own made list of anxiety-provoking triggers and situations, using the relaxation techniques that you learn when necessary.

The ways your psychologist may choose to expose you to your anxiety-inducing thoughts are by, Imaginal exposure – you will be asked to imagine your anxiety-provoking triggers, In vivo exposure – you will be asked to face your anxiety triggers directly, for example, if you have social anxiety disorder then you may be asked to give a short speech in front of the audience, Virtual reality exposure – using technology to combine elements of imaginary and in vivo exposure, proven especially helpful for soldiers and other who suffer from the post-traumatic stress disorder.

3. Dialectical Behavioural Therapy

It is the most effective type of CBT that is used to treat borderline personality disorder. While you are in session during this therapy, you will learn to both accept your anxiety all the while actively working to change it. It is very similar to the notion of loving yourself the way you are, while still trying to change yourself for the better.

You can learn four powerful skills during your treatment. They are,

i. Mindfulness – Learning to live in present and connect with the moment.

ii. Distress tolerance – Learning to manage your anxiety when you are faced with stressful situations.

iii. Interpersonal effectiveness—Learning how to say no or ask for what you need.

iv. Emotion regulation – Learning to manage anxiety before they get out of control.

4. Acceptance and Commitment Therapy

In this therapy, you learn to accept the things that are happening to you. Before your anxious thoughts take a toll on your body, your mind accepts the feeling and in turn downsize the effects of the same. It teaches you to value yourself and try sticking in your life commitments and not to let any other feeling take that away from you.

5. Art Therapy

Newest of its kind, researchers are still looking into the effectiveness of the therapy. It is a non-verbal therapy, which is mainly experience-oriented. It will involve you to express your emotions and thoughts in the form of a painting, drawing, or sculpting. It can be done using standalone as well as with a combination of various other therapy.

6. Psychoanalytic Therapy

Often anxiety symptoms reflect unconscious conflicts, according to the Freudian model. The primary purpose of this therapy to resolve them. In this method of a therapy session, you and your therapist examine your thoughts, desires, and fears to better understand how you view yourself. With that knowledge, try to reduce the cause and effect of the same. It is not a quick solution therapy; it is one of the most intensive forms of therapy and it may take years to identify patterns in your way of thinking.

7. Interpersonal Therapy

This therapy mainly focuses on social roles and personal relationships. In this therapy you work with your therapist to identify any interpersonal issues you may have, past or in present, such as unresolved grief, conflicts with family or friends, and the personal problem with someone, and a major change in work or life role. Once identifying the problem, you will then learn some healthy ways to express emotions and ways to improve your communication with others.

With that knowledge in various types of therapy used by psychologists, let us now try to see how you can make most out of your therapy sessions. Whenever your body and mind change it can be very challenging. However, if you are persistent, determined, and focus, you should see significant improvements. Here below mentioned are the few ways following which you can make most out of your therapy sessions.

- Do not pretend to be OK.
- Ask questions, plenty of questions.
- Tell your therapist anything and everything.
- Do the work outside your sessions.
- Focus on your goals.

- Practice healthy lifestyle choices.

- Make sure you have a social support system.

- Reduce stress in your life that makes your anxiety worse.

Apart from that, if you have anything that you would like to add for yourself, please feel free to add them below in the space provided.

____

____

____

____

____

____

____

____

____

____

____

____

____

____

You cannot decide to seek help and see a consultant, pronto. It will take time to make such tough decisions. But you can set a time frame for yourself while taking a decision. Some of the reasons because of which people often take much time than required to seek help are mentioned below, do not be one of them.

1. "People who go to counseling are crazy. I am not."

Asking for help is a sign of maturity, self-awareness, and possession of a sense of inner strength. Do not hesitate, go for it.

2. "I would rather talk to my friends."

Yes, you can, and you must talk to your friends. Therapy does not supplant friendship, as a friend cannot do the work of a psychotherapist. Therapists are trained in their field. It is also important that you have more than a supportive friend as support is not the only concern of a therapist. There is more to it. Therapist challenges you, listen to you, based on the experiences they gave you some task to perform and help you analyze yourself.

3. "I wouldn't even know what to talk about."

Relax, you do not have to know anything to talk about. I train your therapist in such areas, they will break the ice and you just need to follow up. Try taking a session and this fear will automatically go away.

4. "I cannot afford it."

Sometimes your insurance would not cover for the therapy that is right, but are you willing to sacrifice your next trip in summer and make an investment in yourself? Investing today in therapy will head off much more costly, life-affecting issues in the future.

5. "I don't have time to spare."

This is a problem that will not go away with time on its own, if you do not put in efforts, finding few hours to deal with them now might save you time in coming times, also a bunch of money and heartaches, in the latter part of life.

6. "Receiving counseling is a sign of weakness."

Nothing else apart from this statement is true if you think. It takes a lot of courage to address your problem and resolve them. Taking this bold move is the first step in the progression.

7. "I saw a psychologist once, and it didn't help."

It might have happened to you. But every psychologist is an individual practitioner, so there is no reason to believe that your next therapist would fail you in the same way the previous one did. Try seeking help from another therapist with whom you can better connect.

8. "What good is talking going to do?"

Talking will help you build a network of trust with someone, a person who knows you very well and with whom you can talk to regarding anything. Once you build that relationship with your therapist, you will start to accept and make positive changes that were not possible prior.

9. "I am not comfortable talking to a stranger."

Therapy is a relationship that is professional and personal at the same time. The kind of alliance you form with your counselor is a crucial factor in your treatment. Most of the therapists are skilled to make you feel comfortable in the first few minutes of talking. The best part is, if you do not feel comfortable, you can still tell the same thing to your therapist as well.

10. "They only care about money and not my feelings."

I have read no name in Forbes' list who is a professional psychologist. Most of the therapists choose this career to help people, yes earning is a goal, but that is not the only goal. Also, if you search for, there may be some therapist that does not take sessions for money, but to help people with the issue and you can even try talking to them.

Each year in the United States, anxiety disorders affect roughly one in every five adults, according to the National Institution of Mental Health. Still, there are plenty of misconceptions surrounding these conditions. Every reality is bound with a myth that people have in their head. Anxiety disorders are no different. I list some myths entailing anxiety disorders and facts that set them straight below for you to read. These myths can create stigma and people start to avert seeking help. So, it is very important to know the facts.

Myth: Snap a tuber bank on your wrist every time you have a bad thought.
Fact: Studies show that suppressing your thoughts strengthens them and more frequent. Think of it this way: the thoughts you resist persist.

Myth: If a panic attack gets too bad, you can pass out or lose control.
Fact: It is unlikely you will faint, which is caused by a sudden drop in blood pressure. During a panic attack, your blood pressure does not fall; it rises slightly.

Myth: If you have an anxiety disorder, it is important to avoid stress and situations that make you feel "stressed".
Fact: Treating yourself as if you are fragile and avoiding risk leads to feeling demoralized. Avoiding anxiety reinforces it. You can be anxious and still do whatever you have to do.

Myth: Always carry a paper bag in case you hyperventilate.

Fact: Paper bags can serve as safety crutches that keep you anxious about being anxious. Hyperventilation, while uncomfortable, is not dangerous.

Myth: The causes of anxiety disorders are usually rooted in childhood, so effective therapy must focus on that period.

Fact: Research shows that effective treatment focuses on the here and now, including new skills to manage thoughts, emotions, discomforts, and behavior.

Myth: Medications for anxiety are addictive, so we should take them only if necessary.

Fact: Selective serotonin reuptake inhibitors (SSRI) and Serotonin and norepinephrine reuptake inhibitors (SNRI) antidepressants are not addictive. Benzodiazepines might be helpful in the short term, but they can lead to increased tolerance and dependence after long-term use.

Myth: Medication is the only treatment for anxiety disorders.

Fact: Medication can be effective. But scientific research shows that cognitive-behavioral therapy (CBT) may be just as or more effective than medication for most people, especially in the long run.

Myth: Some people are just worrywarts or neurotic, and there is nothing that can make any difference.

Fact: Therapy can help you reduce worry and suffering and learn a unique relationship to your temperament and how long neurotic habits have been in your life.

Myth: A never-ending supply of compassionate reassurance from family and friends in avoiding stress are good for someone with anxiety problems.

Fact: Well-meaning friends and family can inadvertently get caught up in reassurance compulsions and help maintain fears by keeping you from facing them. Compassionate and kindly encouragement to move through anxiety and doubts, instead of avoiding them, is more helpful.

Takeaways

- Seeking help for your problems from a therapist is not a sign of weakness.
- You do not have to live with your anxiety your entire life. Treatment can help you overcome it. For most of the anxiety problems, therapy is often the most effective option.

- Therapy teaches you the tools to overcome anxiety and gives you a clear picture of how to use them.

- Every reality is bound with a myth that people have in their head. Anxiety disorders are no different. Try not to fall for these stigmas relating to anxiety.

5. Sustenance For Existence

5. Sustenance For Existence

One indeed needs to make a variety of lifestyle alterations when dealing with anxiety. What you eat makes a sizeable difference in your mundane routine. Eating your meal that is high in vegetables, fruits, legumes, lean protein, and whole grains can help you fight your anxiety.

Loss of appetite in one of the major symptoms of anxiety disorder. We must always remember, the food that you eat will provide you nutrients. Nutrients are substances that provide: energy for activity, growth, and all functions of the body such as breathing, digesting food, and keeping warm; materials for the growth and repair of the body, and for keeping the immune system healthy. It is clinically proven that proper nutrition can help you improve your anxiety symptoms.

I am not a nutritionist, but with my research and learning, I would like to share some food you should seriously consider adding to your diet list, if possible, in one way or the other that will help you with your condition are hereby listed. *If you have any questions, concerns, and allergies to nuts or dairy products, please consult your doctor before making your move. The list below are some foods that may help you manage your anxiety feelings; they may not cure or make you anxiety-free. Having these foods in limited quantity in your next diet may help you better control and manage your anxiety.*

1. Brazil nuts

With its high content of selenium, a chemical element that is proven to help in the improvement of mood by reducing inflammation, which is often observed at the highlighted level when your body experiences anxiety. Selenium always works as an antioxidant., which in turn helps prevent cell damage. It prevails antioxidant property because it is rich in vitamin E. Low level of vitamin E in the body may be one of the reasons to get your anxious thoughts to trigger.

Also, too much selenium can cause side effects. The upper limit for selenium for an adult is 400 micrograms (mcg) per day. So be careful not to take supplements with high dosage or eat more than three Brazil nuts a day.

Other various nuts, animal products, and vegetables, such as mushrooms and soybeans, are an excellent source of selenium as well.

2. Fatty fish

What nutrition comes to mind when we think about fish? Omega-3, yes right, omega-3 is a fatty acid that has a direct and strong relationship with cognitive function and mental health. Some fatty fish that have an exorbitant amount of omega-3 are salmon, sardines, mackerel, herring, and trout. Beware to make sure you take omega-3 only, recent research has shown that is a person consumes too much of another kind of fatty acid, such as omega-6, it puts them at higher risk of developing anxiety disorders.

Scientifically, omega-3 rich foods have traces of alpha-linolenic acid (ALA) that comprises two essential fatty acids - eicosapentaenoic acid (EPA), and docosahexaenoic acid (DHA). They both help regulate neurotransmitters, reduce inflammation, and promote healthy brain function.

Various therapists recommend eating at least two servings of fatty fish a week will help reduce self-reported anxiety. Salmon and sardines are among those few fatty acid-rich foods that contain vitamin D. Researchers are increasingly linking vitamin D deficiency to mood disorders, such as depression and anxiety.

3. Eggs

It is common; we know that egg yolks are another dominant source of vitamin D as well. It is an excellent source of protein. Eggs are categorized as a complete protein, meaning it contains all the required amino acids that our body uses for growth and development.

Also, eggs contain tryptophan – an amino acid that helps create serotonin. Serotonin is a chemical neurotransmitter that helps our body to regulate sleep, mood, memory, and behaviour. It is also proven to improve brain functionality and alleviate anxiety.

4. Pumpkin seeds

Enriches with potassium – that helps regulate electrolyte balance and manage our blood pressure. Pumpkin seed is the right choice for food. Bananas are also potassium-rich that may help you reduce signs of stress and anxiety.

Pumpkin seeds are also an excellent source of the mineral zinc. Research carried out on 100 high school female students resulted in a conclusion that zinc deficiency may negatively affect mood. It is an essential mineral for brain and nerve development. We find the majority of zinc in the brain region that is involved with emotions in our bodies.

5. Dark chocolate

Do not get it confused with the milk chocolate that the majority of people like, here we are talking about the dark chocolate. People tend to hate it because of its bitter taste. A 2014 research found that 40g of dark chocolate helped reduce perceived stress in female students.

Also, dark chocolate and cocoa are found to improve the mood for most people. Many of the research mentioned is observational, it may further require deep study to better interpret.

Chocolate has a high tryptophan content, which our body uses to turn into mood-enhancing neurotransmitters, same as serotonin in the brain. Dark chocolate is also a wonderful source of magnesium. Consuming a diet with enough magnesium in it or taking it as a supplement helps reduce symptoms of depression. It is also rich in polyphenols, specifically, flavonoids. Flavonoids help reduce neuroinflammation and cell death in the brain as well as improve blood flow.

There are so many varieties of dark chocolate available, aim for 70 percent or more. Dark chocolate contains added sugars and fats, so a small serving of 1 to 3 grams (g) is appropriate.

6. Turmeric

It is a spice mostly used in India and South-East Asia. Any recipe is incomplete without turmeric in Indian cuisine. The active ingredient in turmeric is curcumin. Curcumin helps to lower your anxiety by reducing inflammation and oxidative stress that often increases in people experiencing mood disorders or anxiety. Research also resulted in the conclusion that curcumin reduces anxiety in obese adults.

You can easily make turmeric a healthy part of your next meal, it has minimal flavour, so can be added to any dishes, such as curries, casserole dishes, or even smoothie.

7. Chamomile

Chamomile tea is consumed by many people around the globe, it is an herbal remedy because of its anti-inflammatory, antibacterial, antioxidant, and relaxant properties. It is useful in managing your anxiety. It is easily available, and you can freely consume high doses of it without worrying. It is herbal and so it does not have any side effects.

Chamomile flowers have flavonoids present in it. Study shows that it helps reduce anxiety symptoms. However, there are no signs of preventing new episodes of anxiety from chamomile.

8. Yogurt

It contains healthful bacteria, Lactobacillus and Bifidobacteria. There are emerging traces that these bacteria and fermented products have positive effects on brain health. It is not a choice for vegan, but the recent clinical review shows that yogurt and other dairy products may also produce an anti-inflammatory effect in the body. Research shows that fermented foods reduce social anxiety in some young people, also consuming healthful bacteria increases happiness in some people.

Adding yogurt and other fermented food to your next diet can benefit the natural gut bacteria and may reduce anxiety and stress. Other fermented food may include cheese, kimchi, sauerkraut, and fermented soy products.

9. Green tea

With its richness in an amino acid called theanine, which is receiving increasing scrutiny because of its potential effects on mood disorders. Theanine has anti-anxiety and calming effects and may increase the production of serotonin and dopamine. Green tea can be easily added to the day-to-day diet. If it is possible try to substitute it in place of soft drinks, coffee, and alcoholic beverages.

Study shows that consume 200mg of theanine improved self-reported relaxation and calmness while reducing tension in the body.

10. Avocado

They are rich in stress-relieving B vitamins and heart-healthy fat that helps reduce anxiety. Avocado also has vitamin E, a nutrient that is important for vision, reproduction, and maintaining healthy skin. It is also related to cognition, helps widen blood vessels, and is needed for the formation of red blood cells. Because vitamin E is fat soluble, we only find it in foods like nuts and avocados that have high-fat content.

Avocado can be consumed raw in a salad or make guacamole out of it. Avocado can be easily mixed with various other ingredients to make smoothies. Avocado ice-cream? Yes, have it occasionally, take care of your fat intake as well.

List of various other foods that might help you alleviate anxiety, and its effect is,

Spinach and Swiss chard contain magnesium. It may help you to ease anxiety. Aim for whole foods, vegetables, fruit, legumes, whole grains, lean meats, and especially fish. Nuts, especially almonds, are an excellent source of vitamin E. Vitamin E deficiency has been linked to mood disorders. Chia seeds are also a superb source of omega-3s. Cinnamon is another good spice that helps reduce inflammation in your body.

Eat a varied and balanced diet with high quality, nutrient-dense carbohydrates, fats, and proteins.

Takeaways

- A healthy diet should provide all the nutrients needed for healthy brain function.
- The diet that contains antioxidant and anti-inflammatory compounds, also vitamins and minerals, may help you reduce inflammation and oxidative stress.

- Limit your high intake on sugar, salt, and fat, especially trans fats, might help reduce inflammation. Get to minimum utilization of alcohol and coffee as these may increase episodes of anxiety and the associated symptoms.

- Most of the research relating to food helps our body to reduce stress and anxiety is at very early stages of development. Consult your doctor or nutritionist before making your first move.

6. Need Prescription?

6. Need Prescription?

"Drugs do not cure anxiety."

Drugs do not cure anxiety; they only help you to manage its symptoms, so that you can function best and carry on with your day-to-day routine.

Medication can help you in the short run. Do not get addicted to it. I would suggest you follow some home remedies, physical exercises, and yoga that we have discussed in the previous chapter to help with anxiety and its symptoms, keep medications as your last resort if possible.

Many types of medications are available. Because every person is unique, you and your doctor may have to try several medications to find the right one for you.

Do not start to take any medicines or drugs discussed in this chapter without consulting your doctor. I have mentioned all drugs that are available in the market for information purposes only. I do not promote or sell any kinds of products to you.

1. Benzodiazepines

These are sedatives that can help relax your muscles and calm your mind. They increase the effects of certain neurotransmitters, which are chemicals that relay messages between your brain cells. Benzodiazepines help in treating many kinds of anxiety disorders, including panic disorders, generalized anxiety disorder (GAD), and social anxiety disorder.

There are various drugs available in the market that contain benzodiazepines content, some of them are,

- alprazolam (Xanax)
- chlordiazepoxide (Librium)
- clonazepam (Klonopin)
- diazepam (Valium)
- lorazepam (Ativan)

Also, it increases drowsiness and causes problems with balance and memory, be advised to not keep using these drugs for a longer time. They can also be habit-forming. It is very important to only use these kinds of drugs under your doctor's prescription only.

Side effects

We already discussed two drowsiness and memory problems, apart from that taking benzodiazepines can also cause confusion, vision impairment, headaches, and feelings of depression. If you have started taking a benzodiazepine regularly for over two weeks, it is important not to stop the pills intake suddenly, as this could cause a seizure in some people. Be advised to talk to your doctor about slowly tapering off your dosage to reduce your risk of seizure to minimality.

2. Buspirone

It is used to treat both short-term as well as chronic anxiety disorders. Although, not completely understood its working, but it is thought to affect chemicals in the brain that regulate mood. It can take up to several weeks to become effective in your body. It is available as a generic drug and the brand-name drug as Buspar.

Side effects

Common side effects may include headaches, dizziness, sleeping problems, nausea, feeling too much nervous or too excited. Some people also reported strange dreams while sleeping when taking buspirone.

3. Antidepressants

It works by affecting neurotransmitters. These drugs are used to treat anxiety symptoms. They might take four to six weeks before you observe noticeable effects and changes.

There are different antidepressants, let us see some of them that are most used.

i. SSRIs

Selective serotonin reuptake inhibitors (SSRIs) increase levels of serotonin, a neurotransmitter that affects mood, sexual desire, appetite, sleep, and memory in your body. They are often prescribed starting with a low dose and then later doctors will escalate your dosage.

Examples of SSRIs that are used to treat anxiety are,

- escitalopram (Lexapro)
- fluoxetine (Prozac)
- paroxetine (Paxil)
- sertraline (Zoloft)

Side effects

It can cause a variety of side effects, but most people tolerate them very well. Some side effects may include nausea, dry mouth, weakness in muscles, dizziness, sexual dysfunction, and diarrhea.

ii. Tricyclics

These works, and SSRIs, do for treating most anxiety disorders, except obsessive-compulsive disorder (OCD). It is working the same as SSRIs, starting with reduce dose and then later increasing it gradually.

Examples of tricyclics used for anxiety include,

- clomipramine (Anafranil)
- imipramine (Tofranil)

Tricyclics are used less often nowadays as newer drugs compared to tricycles show fewer side effects on our body.

Side effects

Side effects of tricyclics include dizziness, drowsiness, lack of energy, and dry mouth. They can also include nausea and vomiting, constipation, blurred vision, and weight gain.

iii. MAOIs

Monoamine oxidase inhibitors (MAOIs) increases the number of neurotransmitters that regulate mood. It is used to treat panic disorder and social phobia.

Some of the MAOIs that are FDA-approved to treat depression but used off-label for anxiety is hereby mentioned below,

- isocarboxazid (Marplan)
- phenelzine (Nardil)
- selegiline (Emsam)
- tranylcypromine (Parnate)

Side effects

Same as tricyclics, MAOIs are older drugs that cause quite more number of side effects than newer drugs available. MAOIs tags along with several restrictions, like you can not consume cheese and red wine while you are taking these drugs. Having so can dangerously increase your blood pressure and cause other potentially life-threatening side effects.

4. Beta-blockers

Mostly used to treat heart conditions. They are often used off-label to help relieve the physical symptoms of anxiety, especially in social anxiety disorder.

Some doctors may prescribe a beta-blocker such as propranolol (Inderal) to help reduce your anxiety symptoms in stressful situations, such as attending a party or giving a speech. Consuming these drugs in every situation may build up a habit and every time you are in stressful situations, your body may demand beta-blockers.

Side effects

They rarely cause side effects in everyone, but some potential side effects include fatigue, drowsiness, dry mouth, shortness of breath, nausea, and sometimes even trouble sleeping.

Takeaways

- Drugs can not cure anxiety; they can give you a push.
- There are so many medications available to help you ease your anxiety feelings, you need to consult your doctor before making your first move.

- Try not to or limit your usage in drugs to feel better in anxious situations, rather than opt for other methods, such as exercise, yoga, and various other techniques we have discussed in prior chapters.

- Every drug has its side effect on our body, at least most of them. So, if you observe or feel any affects urgently consult your doctor first-hand.

7. Working Out With Numbers

7. Working Out With Numbers

If statistics and numbers mean nothing to you, you can skip this chapter. Still, I would advise you to read it once. This chapter does not have a direct link to strategies under anxiety, but instead, it is for understanding some real-word data. Numbers are the best form of representation of any kind. We will see the real-world data produced by the *Institute for Health Metrics and Evaluation* and reported in their flagship *Global Burden of Disease* study. All data shown are of 2017, that is the latest and most accurate data that we have available currently.

For 2017, this study estimates that 792 million people lived with a mental health disorder. This is slightly over one in ten people globally (10.7%). Share of males : females are 9.3% male and 11.9% female.

People suffering from anxiety disorder contributes 3.8% of the global population varying between 2.5% - 7% in different countries. Globally an estimated 284 million people experienced an anxiety disorder in 2017, making it the most prevalent mental health or neurodevelopmental disorder. Around 63 percent (179 million) were female, relative to 105 million males.

(All the data shown are of 2017)

Top 5 countries with the highest percentage of people experiencing anxiety disorders.

1. New Zealand – 8.54%

2. Norway – 7.59%

3. Northern Ireland – 7.46%

4. Iran – 6.90%

5. Australasia – 6.88%

Top 5 countries with the highest percentage of females suffering from various anxiety disorders.

1. New Zealand – 10.82%

2. Northern Ireland – 9.44%

3. Norway – 9.36%

4. France – 8.99%

5. Uruguay – 8.89%

Top 5 countries with a maximum fraction of males experience anxiety disorders.

1. New Zealand – 6.08%

2. Norway – 5.83%

3. Iran – 5.41%

(All the data shown are of 2017)

4. Northern Ireland – 5.41%

5. Australasia – 5.09%

Top 5 countries that have shown maximum improvement in the drop of anxiety disorders patient population.

1. Canada – 7%

2. Columbia – 4%

3. China – 3%

4. East Asia – 3%

5. Qatar – 3%

The United States is in the 6th position in the list of countries with globally affected people with anxiety disorder with 6.64%, whereas India is at the 150th position with 3.3%.

Top 5 countries with the maximum number of anxiety patients in the age category of 5 – 14 years.

1. Norway – 6.91%

2. Northern Ireland – 6.72%

3. New Zealand – 6.38%   *(All the data shown are of 2017)*

4. Germany – 6.34%

5. Netherlands – 6.29%

Top 5 countries with the maximum number of anxiety patients in the age category of 15 – 19 years.

1. New Zealand – 10.11%

2. Norway – 9.99%

3. Northern Ireland – 9.90%

4. Netherlands – 8.82%

5. France – 8.69%

Top 5 countries with the maximum number of anxiety patients in the age category of 20 – 24 years.

1. New Zealand – 10.79%

2. Norway – 8.85%

3. Australasia – 8.83%

4. Iran – 8.76%

5. Northern Ireland – 8.69%

Top 5 countries with the maximum number of anxiety patients in the age category of 25 – 29 years.

1. New Zealand – 11.08%

(All the data shown are of 2017)

2. Iran – 9.11%

3. Australasia – 8.98%

4. Australia – 8.63%

5. United States – 8.24%

Top 5 countries with the maximum number of anxiety patients in the age category of 25 – 29 years.

1. New Zealand – 11.16%

2. Iran – 9.23%

3. Australasia – 8.95%

4. United States – 8.67%

5. Australia – 8.61%

Top 5 countries with the maximum number of anxiety patients in the age category of 30 – 69 years.

1. Norway – 8.19%

2. Northern Ireland – 8.07%

3. New Zealand – 7.91%

4. Iran – 7.63%

5. Brazil – 7.28%

5. Tropical Latin America – 7.28%

(All the data shown are of 2017)

8. Flying Through It

8. Flying Through It

As prevalent as anxiety is, so are its high responsive treatments. Can we tell who will get better and who would not? Well, the answer lies in these below mentioned three "beliefs" they can typically learn at some point of time in their life, the sooner the better, to manage their anxiety symptoms.

1. Believe it's time you need change.

You have already done what you need to; it is not helping, and still, you are stuck at one point. It is time you start doing something else that you have not tried. This book spoke about various ways in which you can feel better and start to alleviate your anxiety. Accept, it is the time you need to change to a novel approach and start to follow the same.

2. Believe in the strategies you learned in this book.

Start to implement all the strategies and apply your knowledge that you gained from this book and you will get results. Self-doubt and second-guessing the process is only a distraction from building the new habits that will take you away from anxiety and towards greater calm.

3. Believe nothing is stagnant, you are bound to grow.

Trust yourself, nothing in this world has remained forever, nor this feeling will. People just like you all over the world have experienced anxious patterns yet found sustained peace of mind, so why do you think you could not? Know yourself and believe in yourself, you are bound to gain control over your anxiety.

What could be your biggest challenges at this point in reading the book? Perhaps you continue to struggle and have not yet seen any noticeable benefit. Or perhaps the improvements feel very negligible and not impactful enough. It can feel impractical to keep believing in yourself and your treatment approach when you are not noticing any measurable change. It is time you start to address some questions to try to understand why it is not helping you. Ask yourself these questions and try to answer them in your mind or space provided.

Were you able to follow strategies that this book talks about?

____

____

____

____

____

Do you believe in yourself and that some of the positive changes can help you towards gaining success?

How long you feel there are no changes after you started to follow what this book teaches?

____

____

____

____

____

____

____

____

____

____

____

Give yourself compassion for going towards what is difficult, and for not giving up. Always remember, the road to progress is not always straight. Change might not unfold in a straight line always, although we at times believe it should, that is why when we confront setbacks, we become self-critical and start to doubt ourselves. This thinking sabotages your progress and contributes to the feeling of giving up entirely.

The truth is that setbacks and failures along the path of success are inevitable for everyone. Our brains have the miraculous ability to reconfigure, to grow, and to make changes; however, our brain also clings to what has become our habit over the years. This contradiction leads to the conclusion that change does not come immediately or without efforts. Sustained change, the kind of change that makes a difference, takes time and consistency.

Each time you find yourself in a difficult situation and feel like you have hit a roadblock, instead of self-criticism and self-defeat, consider the roadblock an alarming signal of your growth and progress. When progress on the anxiety-reduction trail stalls, or even halts completely, it means you have likely progressed more than you imagined, and that is why the setback bothers you. Setbacks are part of your brain's adjustment process. Keep persisting, never give up, and return to the strategies again and again. It will pay off.

Gather all strength and refocus on the bigger picture in which overall strategies are important to you in maintaining your less-anxious life. These are a list of strategies that either worked very well for you or are lined to something you care about, such as active social life. Here is the list of some things that I would suggest you keep in mind.

- Physical exercise
- Daily mindfulness
- Physical health
- Live your best life
- Acceptance
- Challenge your thoughts
- Exposure
- Make space for yourself separate from your anxious thoughts

Likewise, you can make your list in the space provided below.

____

____

____

____

____

____

____

____

____

____

____

____

Building your support network.

Establishing a reliable support network outside of your medical or psychological treatment team is a very crucial step while managing your mental health. Your support network might include family members, close friends, trusted clergy, or community leaders.

You can start to invite people in your network by disclosing your condition and by asking if they would be willing to offer support in ways that respect their personal boundaries and obligations. It is in best practice if you choose people that,

- You trust
- You have a close relationship with
- Have the traits you desire in a supportive person, such as being empathetic, caring, or a good listener

If you do not have many relationships that you feel comfortable asking to be in your support network, look for some online or in-person support group in your locality or town. A support group will help you connect with peers who may experience similar struggles. Most times we feel most comfortable talking to others who are going through similar challenges in life, people who understand and "get" where you are coming from.

Social Support

Increasing social support will help you to improve your moods, behaviour, and relationships. It will also help to improve communication and feelings of connectedness.

You may find it difficult at first to break the ice and talk to others regarding the problems that you are facing, but trust me, once you start then you will realize you should have done it sooner.

You can start building your social support by following simple steps.

- Make a list of people who might be open to a visit or a phone call when:
    - You need support
    - You need help with solving problems
    - You need encouragement to improve your mood
- Purchase some inexpensive invitations or make some at home.
- Give or mail the invitations to the people on your list.
- For local support groups
- For specialized support groups

Take Time to Connect with Others

Spent maximum time with your spouse or partner. You can set aside time each day to reconnect, even if you sit together for a cup of coffee together in the morning or quiet conversation in your garden in the evening. The time spent together while watching television or attending a guest at home is not accounted for it. Make sure you spend time talking to each other that both feel good about.

You must always find time to do other things than just your work, like reading books or spending time with your children. If you are a teen, go for a bike ride in the evening or spend quality time with your grandparents.

Keep yourself connected to friends by joining them for a coffee occasionally, a monthly book club, or a night out. Build your support community, especially if you are a single parent. Start with a simple one or two activities a month, then add more than you get comfortable and find more time.

Take care of your emotional and spiritual needs. If you like talking to a therapist or clergy member, do it. If you like to practice yoga, attend a spiritual community, write, paint, read poetry, write a journal, do it. Do what works for you the best and do that helps you.

Something for the parents

If you are the parent of a child with mental health issues, it is natural to feel isolated sometimes, even when surrounded by a team of caregivers and professionals. Navigate through online resources and find websites that offer ways to connect with other parents whose children are going through with similar conditions. Team up with them, talk to each other. Both you and the person in front will feel better. There are various government and non-government websites available to search for the same.

Educate Your Family

It is common to have depression, anxiety, ADHD, and other mental health conditions. They are not the result of a lack of coping ability or personal strength. Do not hesitate or feel bad about what you are facing and be bold to talk to your family about it.

A person with mental health problems is suffering from serious issues, they are not trying to make symptoms up. What looks like laziness or crossness at before may be signs of depression. What may seem like being a dramatic or over-the-top reaction to us at first can be symptoms of anxiety.

Often mental health conditions are hereditary. Knowing this may help other family members to better understand your situation and symptoms.

Identify Your Team

Is there anyone you can call any time of the day?

The person you can call when you need to vent about work, family, or emotional stress is the right fit to be on your team. During stressful times, fill them in and ask if they can reach out to you regularly to help you feel supported.

Who can keep you focused while at work?

They might be your colleagues or peers you can count on for additional support and to help keep you focused while at work. Often, personal struggles in these conditions can negatively affect your performance at work without you even realizing it. It is very important to have someone at the workplace you can check in with, someone who can help you get back on track if you are struggling.

Any professor or school/university staff that can help?

It can be your professor who understands school/college advisors, or other staff members that can communicate with you regularly and are available for your support. It is very important to find someone who can communicate anything to your parents as well while you face any problems. Make sure you provide them with your parents' work and personal phone numbers.

Addressing these three questions and finding the right people that will be on your team is a crucial step. Make sure you have enough people from various places so that you feel connected and continue to get support wherever you are.

Manage and keep a folder with the following mentioned information somewhere handy. This will allow you to advocate for appropriate services by having important information at hand.

- A list of all medical providers, mental health providers, and others involved in providing care and support. Include names, phone numbers, and addresses.
- A list of medications
- Educational records
- Medical history

In the space provided below, write the names and contact information of people that you have to choose to be on your team.

____

____

____

____

____

Support groups

For some people, group therapy is more impactful than individual therapy. It is extremely effective in lessening anxiety symptoms. Group therapy works best because it challenges your ideas that you are alone in suffering and are somehow "worse" or "less than" others as a result. This experience also reduces shame and isolation and helps to accept anxiety while you continue to live your normal life parallelly.

In most cases, people develop self-awareness around their role in social relationships while connecting to people in group therapy. While in the group, a person may act out a role that they use to manage their anxiety in actual life, i.e., overly friendly, withdrawn, very inquisitive, constantly talking, dismissive. Group members typically reflect on the roles they notice and provide one another with feedback. As group therapy is not real life and is confidential, it feels safe for people to process such feedbacks. As an outcome, they become more flexible or even adopt other roles in the group that will eventually extend to their real-life relationships.

We already know by now, when we are in an anxious state, adrenaline can take over. It can be hard at times to know what we feel deep down, let alone find the words to express what we are feeling. Yet, anxiety decreases when we talk to others present around us. Group therapy is a type of exposure where you will feel anxious at times.

At the same time, it is a non-threatening place for you to become more skilful at knowing what you are feeling when you are feeling, and becoming comfortable expressing the same to others.

Finding a group

If you are firm and decided that group therapy is a treatment approach you would like to try, and you have a therapist, consider asking them if they know of a group that would be a good fit for you. Alternatively, there is a "Find a Support Group" feature available on the Anxiety and Depression Association of America website and the Psychology Today website. Be sure to look them up and search for a support group in your town.

Remember and keep in mind that there are two common types of group therapies. "Process-oriented" groups are led by a therapist, but generally, the therapist lets the group members steer the discussion. Process groups are about the group members' experiences of what they are observing, feeling, or want to discuss.

Another is "Psycho-educational" groups also are led by a therapist, but the therapist takes on an instructor role. Psychoeducational groups are helpful when you are looking to gain specific skills in some areas of your life or problems that you are facing. In this case, an anxiety psychoeducational group might discuss coping skills and strategies.

Starting a group

We know and have seen anxiety is an extremely prevalent issue for many people. If you are looking for an anxiety therapy group in your locality feasible to you and cannot find one, chances are others are, too. If you decide to start a group, think carefully about how you wish to structure it, what kinds of members you are targeting for the group, for example, would you like to have people with only anxiety problems, relationship problems, or in general with various mental health conditions? Finding a leader is an important task too for the group to function properly. You would want it to be figured out whether you want your group to be process-oriented or psycho-educational. It is also very important to think and set some primary group therapy rules. Do not try to squeeze in people you already know like your family members or friends as it will reduce anonymity and the comfort that comes from anonymity. Confidentiality among group members is the key to feeling safe and open, which is the key that helps people grow in group therapy. The place is another concern, to start a group therapy you need place depending on how many numbers of people you are targeting. Setting the right group meeting day and time is also very important as we would like to gather as many people as we could.

Once you have things figured out you can start your own group. if you are planning to do this for your community

134

or town, please know that is the best step you are taking for yourself and for the people who are going to be benefited from it.

Staying on the course

Just like many things in life, success in your pursuit of anxiety reduction and internal peace takes patience, adaptability, and perseverance. No questions, hands down. Anxiety is unpleasant, and you would like it to stop at this moment or as quickly as possible.

However, building habits take practice to form and they take practice to break. Compassionately remind yourself that there is nothing wrong with you if you feel that your recovery is not moving as fast as you would like. And just because it is taking time does not mean you will not get better. You will, it just takes time.

Believe in yourself and allow yourself to adjust strategies for your personal brand of anxiety symptoms. One strategy may work for a while, but it is important to try new ones, so you stay challenged and keep growing. As your symptoms improve with time, the anxiety will probably change and present itself differently which you might not have experienced before. You will constantly need to adjust and bring new skills into your repertoire. If any strategy is not working or going only so far, then consider individual psychotherapy or group therapy, whichever you find comfortable. You may even try to do both and decide for yourself. Continuing both at the same time is also advisable. If you think therapy is not working on its own, consider combining psychotherapy and medication, while you continue to practice various strategies that we discussed in this book. Most importantly, whatever you do, just do not give up!

Allow yourself to pick the work back up again and again. Believe in the process. Your work will pay off in the form of a brighter future.

Always remember, nothing in this world has ever remained forever, everything is in motion, this shall pass too.

9. Case Study

9. Case Study

Not everyone is having similar effects of anxiety, all of us can have anxiety is in different ways. I have interviewed some people who are suffering from anxiety or who experienced anxiety in the past. Their identity is kept confidential. This chapter will help you to know how anxiety affects others, apart from you.

Let us start with the first interview. This person successfully fought anxiety and is now living a happy life. Learning that worrying about something not in your hands will do no good. Another way worked out for this person was by finding the correct peace of mind from "Bhagavad Gita" - often referred to as the Gita, is a 700-verse Hindu scripture that is part of the epic Mahabharata, commonly dated to the second century BCE. The Gita is set in a narrative framework of a dialogue between Pandava prince Arjuna and his guide and charioteer Krishna. After having a friendly conversation with them, I started asking questions that we want and are curious about.

Author: *"Can you tell me if you have ever seen a mental health professional, such as a psychologist or a psychiatrist?"*

Interviewee: *"Yes, but not for a longer time. Attended like 2-3 sessions."*

Author: *"Can you tell me what psychological problems you have been seen for?"*

Interviewee: *"Depression."*

Author: *"What does your counselor think about you, were you diagnosed with anything?"*

Interviewee: *"I was not diagnosed with anything major, it started with seasonal depression and there were minor signs of the beginning of the persistent depression. So, I had 2-3 sittings with her, and she concluded that I was just overthinking the scenarios that might never take place and stressing myself over them, I was burdening myself with unnecessary pressure and assuming the outcomes of situations that I have not yet stepped into. It affected me more because I felt lonely as I did not talk to anyone at all during that period. I feared being judged by my loved ones, and I thought it did not matter to them if I existed."*

Author: *"Can you tell me if you are currently getting counseling?"*

Interviewee: *"No, I am not seeing them now."*

Author: *"Have you had a period lasting several days or longer when most of the day you felt sad, empty, or anxious?"*

Interviewee: *"Yes, for about 2-3 months."*

Author: *"Have you had a period lasting several days or longer when most of the day you were very discouraged about how things were going in your life?"*

Interviewee: *"Yes, hmm, during the same period of about 2-3 months."*

Author: *"Have you had a period lasting several days or longer when you lost interest in most things you usually enjoy, like work, hobbies, and personal relationships?"*

Interviewee: *"Yes, I lost interest in most of the things I used to love doing. It lasted for about the same period as I was experiencing anxiety."*

Author: *"Would you like to share those experiences, how were you feeling about it?"*

Interviewee: *"[Took a deep breath] So, it began with thinking about certain scenarios and crying in my bed every night... that got me thinking how worthless I am, worthless, I am just a disappointment to people who love me. I used to think about what I am even doing with my life… what if I lose the people who I love because I am worthless and they look down on me. Why would anyone talk to me I am just a failure and disappointment to them nothing else? What if something happens to my parents, what am I going to do, I will have no one left in my life..? I will be all alone. That was my biggest fear, and somewhere deep down it still is. I used to feel no one loves me, not even the people that I thought did. Then I disconnected myself from social life, as you know I love being around people, friends.... I love going to unknown places for food, I stopped doing all that which made me happy. All I would do was just be with myself, sleep in the car during breaks, avoid talking to everyone and anyone. I started getting angry at people for no reason. I am not going anywhere with my career; I have achieved nothing in my life to be proud of."*

Author: *"What makes you feel so sad that nothing could cheer you up for at least several days?"*

Interviewee: *"Just the idea of being lonely that is where everything started from, people not loving me, me not being worthy of their love because I am a failure and just a disappointment to them as I have done nothing worthy to be proud about yet."*

Author: *"Have you had a much smaller appetite than usual?"*

Interviewee: *"Yes, but not for a longer time. It was for a while, a short time before I experienced it."*

Author: *"Have you slept much less than usual?"*

Interviewee: *"Definitely, I used to get proper sleep for only 3-4 hours a day. Was facing difficulty falling asleep and mostly rolling myself on the bed."*

Author: *"What do you think about the future? Is that worry of the future that is causing you anxiety?"*

Interviewee: *"Sometimes thinking about my future develops anxiety, because of the mistakes that I made in the past. About the future, I hope it is significantly better than my past was (fingers crossed) and do something that I can be actually proud of."*

Author: *"Have you studied about physical symptoms of anxiety? If yes, do you experience any?"*

Interviewee: *"I have read about physical symptoms online, but my body was showing no signs of any physical symptoms."*

Author: *"What are some mental symptoms you possess while you are experiencing anxiety?"*

Interviewee: *"Various!! To start with sleepless nights! crying if it's too much or overeating and nowadays very rarely getting angry."*

Author: *"Do you feel uncomfortable meeting new people? What is the chief concern in mind at times when you meet new people?"*

Interviewee: *"Um, no. not at all."*

Author: *"Do you take anxiety relief medications?"*

Interviewee: *"No, did not come to that part were medication was the only option."*

Author: *"What worries you the most? What crosses your mind that makes you feel anxious?"*

Interviewee: *"To put it in simple words, professional future, losing my parents, and being lonely."*

Author: *"how did you face your anxiety and overcome it?"*

Interviewee: *"I still sometimes think about it, but to be honest listening to Bhagavad Gita has helped me a lot, sleeping and keeping my mind calm. When I was depressed, one of my friends who I had least expected to be standing by my side, he was there.... He would call me thrice every day. Also, the therapist even though I saw her for 2-3 sitting it helped me a lot but not more than my friend. His being there for me every day just a call away gave me confidence that not everyone in my life thinks I am a failure and I am not as lonely as I think… It makes a difference to people whether I exist!"*

For the next case study, I took notes from an interview with another person who is currently experiencing anxiety. Mostly it is because the patient is feeling isolated and misses parents and family. Doing everything that can be done and fighting through everyday struggles, let us

146

see some important notes that I have brought out from our conversation.

Author: *"Since how long you think you have been feeling this anxiety?"*

Interviewee: *"It started at a tiny scale at the start. Sometimes it overpowers me and there are times I am normal and have no stress of any sort. It is around 3 months now that anxiety has taken a toll on me."*

Author: *"Can you tell me if you have ever seen a mental health professional, such as a psychologist or a psychiatrist?"*

Interviewee: *"I was dealing and handling with my feeling on my own since last week I searched for a therapist and last week I had my first session with my therapist."*

Author: *"So what do you think after the first session, will you be continuing further, or you do not wish to go?"*

Interviewee: *"The first session was mostly about the therapist talking to me and asking various questions so that my therapist gets to know me. I would continue 3-4 more sessions until I finally make my decision to continue or switch to anything else."*

Author: *"Have you had a period lasting several days or longer when most of the day you felt sad, empty, or anxious?"*

Interviewee: *"Most of the time these feelings stay with me for days or at times, for a week. I get back to my normal life until I suddenly start to feel anxious again."*

Author: *"Have you had a period lasting several days or longer when most of the day you were very discouraged about how things were going in your life?"*

Interviewee: *"Yes, at times when I am anxious."*

Author: *"Have you had a period lasting several days or longer when you lost interest in most things you usually enjoy, like work, hobbies, and personal relationships?"*

Interviewee: *"Umm. Yeah, I usually just like to stay in my bed and do not want to do anything when I experience it."*

Author: *"Would you like to share those experiences, how were you feeling about it?"*

Interviewee: *"I wake up every day in the morning thinking I will remain as positive as I could today, I try very hard to keep reminding myself every morning. But still the thought of me having to do everything alone start to lower my motivation. Right from having to have breakfast alone keeps me thinking, why I could not be with my family. My partner stays in a different town and the situation is such that my partner cannot live with me 24x7 now. When I am anxious, I cannot perform any task, not even the one that I love doing in the first place. I feel why every bad thing only happens to me!"*

Author: *"Have you seen any sign of physical symptoms on your body due to anxiety?"*

Interviewee: *"At times, because of anxiety, I tend to get lipoma under my skin on my hand and thighs. It is mostly harmless. Shortening of breath is another symptom I notice when I feel anxious."*

Author: *"What mental symptoms you think you possess because of anxiety?"*

Interviewee: *"Hehe, honestly, I think I possess all the mental symptoms that are in the world out there while I experience anxiety. I have sleepless nights, I feel very tense and nervous, everything seems like going away from me and the feeling of that void kills me from within."*

Author: *"Do you notice a loss of appetite?"*

Interviewee: *"Yes, generally I skip meals if there is no one to tell me. Most of the time my partner makes sure that I have a proper meal and on time."*

Author: *"What do you think about the future? Is that worry of the future that is causing you anxiety?"*

Interviewee: *"At times, yes, but mostly it is what present that bothers me, I have to live all by myself as my parents and family are back in my home country. Having no one by my side and missing them is what I worry about the most. The only thought about the future I get is, I wish I want to make things better in the future."*

Author: *"Do you feel uncomfortable meeting new people? What is the major concern in mind at times when you meet new people?"*

Interviewee: *"No, I am totally fine meeting new people. But I rarely make friends faster, it takes time for me to build a relationship."*

Author: *"Do you take anxiety relief medications?"*

Interviewee: *"I rather believe in other self-approaches that make me feel better and talking to my partner and therapist helps. Medication can help you push throughout the day, but that is not something I look forward to."*

Author: *"What worries you the most? What crosses your mind that makes you feel anxious?"*

Interviewee: *"The feeling of not having anyone to pamper me all the time is one thing that crosses my mind every time I feel anxious. I tend to miss my parents and home. I feel I want someone to be there with me all the time when I feel this and take care, pamper me."*

Author: *"How you are handling and dealing with your anxiety now?"*

Interviewee: *"I talk to my partner about it. Also, as I mentioned earlier, I have started to take therapy sessions and look forward to gaining positive results. I write, I maintain my journal and write whatever crosses my mind. At times, I write poems as well. With that even, I am thinking to publish my fictional debut novel book shortly."*

Last, we will see a case study about my interview with a person who thinks to have anxiety at a tiny scale, we can say in a very early stage. We will try now to understand how they are feeling and how things appear at a very early stage of anxiety.

Author: *"Can you tell me if you have ever seen a mental health professional, such as a psychologist or a psychiatrist?"*

Interviewee: *"No! I do not think I need it right now."*

Author: *"Have you had a period lasting several days or longer when most of the day you felt sad, empty, or anxious?"*

Interviewee: *"No, I do not think I have experienced much about it."*

Author: *"Have you had a period lasting several days or longer when most of the day you were very discouraged about how things were going in your life?"*

Interviewee: *"Yes, but I would say for some days and not for a longer period."*

Author: *"Would you like to share those experiences, how were you feeling about it?"*

Interviewee: *"[Thinking for a while] Umm, I do not know how it will sound but I feel as if nothing is falling into the right place even after my continuous efforts. In whatever I do, I face failure. I always wonder when will my first thing to go as I have wished. When I put in everything I have and still get nothing as a result I felt tense and lose courage."*

Author: *"What makes you feel so sad that nothing could cheer you up for at least several days?"*

Interviewee: *"Mainly professional setbacks, I would say."*

Author: *"Have you had a much smaller appetite than usual?"*

Interviewee: *"No, I similar to before."*

Author: *"Have you slept much less than usual?"*

Interviewee: *"Yes, tension and worries make me look at starts until late at night."*

Author: *"What are some mental symptoms you possess while you are experiencing anxiety?"*

Interviewee: *"Two major mental symptoms I face is loss of interest in things around me and liveliness I used to have before."*

Author: *"Do you take anxiety relief medications?"*

Interviewee: *"No! that is not what I need right now."*

Author: *"How you are handling and dealing with your anxiety now?"*

Interviewee: *"I try to do better with each day passing, I now focus on enjoying the process rather than the outcome. I am pretty positive that eventually, everything will fall back onto its place."*

Resources

Anxiety and Depression Association of America (adaa.org)

Social Anxiety Institute (socialanxietyinstitute.org)

American Psychological Association (apa.org)

National Alliance on Mental Illness (nami.org)

National Institute of Mental Health (nimh.nih.gov)

National Suicide Prevention Lifeline (1-800-273-8255)

For getting more information browse through (healthline.com), Healthline Media is a Red Ventures Company. © 2005 – 2020.

You can also follow this book's official Instagram account @makingpeacewithanxiety

About the Author

Varsh Patel is a computer science graduate engineer and a technophile. This is his debut book, "Making Peace With Anxiety", a self-help book and a guide to know and better understand anxiety and its symptoms. Varsh is a passionate writer and started with writing poems since his childhood days. When not absorbed in the latest gripping page-turner, Varsh loves cooking, designing graphics, and otherwise spends far too much time at the computer making software for a living.

Follow him on Instagram and Snap Chat: varsh11

Follow him on Facebook: fb.com/pvarsh11